Monologues for Kids and Tweens II

100 New Comedy and Drama Monologues for Young Actors

D1069322

Monologues for Kids and Tweens II

100 New Comedy and Drama Monologues for Young Actors

Mike Kimmel
Foreword by Ben McCain

ISBN 13: 9781953057037
Library of Congress Control Number 2021900323

Monologues for Kids and Tweens II:
100 New Comedy and Drama Monologues for Young Actors
The Young Actor Series: Book 7

Ben Rose Creative Arts
New York - Los Angeles

Printed in the United States of America
First Edition

Publisher's Cataloging-in-Publication Data
provided by Five Rainbows Cataloging Services

Names: Kimmel, Mike, author. | McCain, Ben, writer of foreword.
Title: Monologues for kids and tweens II : 100 new comedy and drama monologues for young actors / Mike Kimmel ; [foreword by] Ben McCain.
Description: Los Angeles : Ben Rose Creative Arts, 2021. | Series:
    Young actor, bk. 7. | Summary: Monologues for Kids and Tweens II is a
    collection of 100 new comedy and drama scripts for young performers. |
    Audience: Grades 2-8.
Identifiers: LCCN 2021900323 (print) | ISBN 978-1-953057-03-7 (paperback) |
    ISBN 978-1-953057-04-4 (ebook : epub) | ISBN 978-1-953057-05-1 (ebook : mobi)
Subjects: LCSH: Monologues--Juvenile literature. | Acting–Auditions–Juvenile
    literature. | Comedy--Juvenile literature. | Drama–Juvenile literature. | BISAC:
    JUVENILE NONFICTION / Performing Arts / General. | YOUNG ADULT
    NONFICTION / Performing Arts / General. | PERFORMING ARTS /
    Monologues & Scenes. | PERFORMING ARTS / Acting & Auditioning.
Classification: LCC PN2080 .K56 2021 (print) | LCC PN2080 (ebook) | DDC
    812/.6–dc23.

Interior design by Booknook.biz

Praise for
Monologues for Kids and Tweens II

"*Monologues for Kids and Tweens II* is spot-on! Where were books like this when I was that age? This gives a young person looking to audition for a school play or local theatre the material to prepare!"

~ Chuck Disney
   Feature Film Producer
   Film Resource Coordinator
   Arizona Film Office, Buckeye, Arizona

"It can be difficult finding a strong monologue. Mike Kimmel has, yet again, provided a source that gives kids and tweens a variety of fun and diverse options."

~ Will Wallace
   Producer, Director, Actor, and Acting Coach
   The Will Wallace Acting Company
   Reagan, The Thin Red Line, I Am Sam, Trafficked, Krispr, The Tree of Life, Rough Riders, The Great Alaskan Race, Leverage, Beverly Hills 90210, Baywatch, The Tempest

"This is the monologue book we've all been searching for! As an artist/educator, I find myself seeking material for young actors that will engage and challenge them intellectually, emotionally, and socially. Times are changing, and the need for art that promotes self-awareness and civility is critical. In his latest book, Kimmel provides monologues curated specifically for the budding young performer. The pieces are short and easy to memorize with positive themes (which makes them perfect for performing or auditioning) while simultaneously leaving space for subtext and deep dives into character choices, behaviors, and motives. I tell my students that once you play a character, you never quite look at life the same afterwards; something changes at the core level every time we 'become a different person' through the empathetic process of acting. This exercise of developing a character and exploring why someone says and does the things they do is sacred, especially to the developing mind, which is why I'm so grateful to have this particular book of monologues in my tool box to share with my students."

~ Misty Marshall
 Executive Director, Empowerment thru Arts LLC,
 Advisory Board Member and Lieutenant Governor,
 LA Music Commission
 Sony recording artist and *American Idol* semifinalist

"Marvelous monologues for kids and tweens. They are swiftly paced with an impact. Even though the dialogue flows effortlessly, each monologue is full of depth. They take the audience on a little intellectual journey while remaining age appropriate. Keep inspiring, Mike!"

~ GiGi Erneta
Actress, Radio and TV Host, and Writer
Flag of My Father, When the Bough Breaks, Roswell, New Mexico, VEEP, The Purge, Nashville, The First, Jane the Virgin, Scandal, American Crime, Queen of the South, Scandal, NCIS New Orleans, Dallas, Friday Night Lights, Risen, Veronica Mars

For Madison and Maxwell,
The Mighty M and M Team

"Be worthy your work if you love it;
The king should be fit for the crown;
Stand high as your art, or above it,
And make us look up and not down."

~ Ella Wheeler Wilcox

Table of Contents

Foreword

Mighty Mike Kimmel is my friend. To have a friend, you've got to be one. Mike was a friend to me on the very first day we met. That's right, he was a friend to me, Ben McCain. We were both hired as actors to do a skit with Jay Leno on **The Tonight Show**. It was called the "Me Channel" skit. It was a spoof of a commercial starring all these well-known women promoting a female-themed channel.

Anyway, Mike had already done about fifty skits with Mr. Leno, so Mr. Kimmel knew his way around the set and the lot at NBC Studios. After we taped, he said, "You can get a discount on the NBC merchandise when you are working on the lot. I'm heading over there. You want to join me?" "Sure," I said. So we started walking and talking.

Mighty Mike grew up in the Bronx in New York City and I grew up on a farm near a small town in the Texas Panhandle called Bovina. There are more cows than people around my home town. We also have the fastest dogs in the world because the trees are so far apart. Mike liked my humor and I liked his. So we picked up merchandise at the NBC store. I enjoy buying stuff like coffee cups and knick knacks to send to friends and family just to let them know I am thinking about them when working on a TV or film set. Mike thought that was cool.

Mike then asked me if I would be interested in being a contestant on the game show **To Tell The Truth**. "You would be perfect," he said. I had told him my brother Butch and I were involved in a family farming and cattle operation back in Texas. He said, "That's perfect. They don't want actors, they want people who can say they do something else, and they are gonna pay you a thousand dollars for a few hours' work." I said, "That sounds good to me." I knew my brother would like that too since we made an agreement when we left our TV show in Oklahoma City to move to Los Angeles that all our individual earnings would go into our company account.

Mike walked me across the lot and introduced me to a young lady, Lisa, who was in charge of booking the guests for the game show. Mike didn't have to do this, but he did. He had already appeared on the show and wasn't eligible to be booked again, but that is the kind of guy Mike Kimmel is. He goes the extra mile for people. A few weeks later, I was a guest on *To Tell The Truth*, and I fooled most everybody in the audience acting like I was a make-up artist who developed the instant face lift. A few weeks after that, I received a thousand dollar check to put in our company account. Mike Kimmel was responsible.

A few years later, my brother and I were producing a comedy film called *Killer Tumbleweeds*. It was a lighthearted spoof of the horror film genre. We asked Mike if he would be interested in playing a role as a wrestler being interviewed about tumbleweeds attacking people in Middle America. Mike thought it sounded like fun and agreed to join the cast. This was my first time directing, and Mike could not have been more professional, kind and prepared.

So folks, specifically kids, tweens, and parents of the kids and tweens who have bought this book, this Mike Kimmel guy knows about acting, monologues, how to get jobs, how to help other actors get jobs – and his material is positive. He shines a bright light! He is a life enhancer! I know, because I have witnessed it first hand. You can read, study, and practice his monologues in this book. You can rely upon them for your upcoming auditions. To me, these monologues are so positive – and we all need something positive in our lives right now. I bet the casting director, producer and director will appreciate and respect the material you are sharing with them when you are auditioning. Don't be surprised if someone in the room asks you if that material is from one of Mike Kimmel's monologue books. Mighty Mike Kimmel keeps writing and continues to bless people with his positive messages.

Ben McCain
Los Angeles, CA

Acknowledgments

As always, a million thanks to Mollie, Adele, and Tammy, my three amazing sisters. Their kindness, graciousness, and generosity are beyond description and beyond compare. More importantly, they never gave up on their weird, introspective little brother. They never laughed at his big, bold Hollywood dreams.

Many thanks to Kimberly Bliquez, GiGi Erneta, Sharon Garrison, Kat Kramer, Karen Kramer, Misty Marshall, Erik Beelman, Stephen Bowling, David Breland, Francis Ford Coppola, Chuck Disney, Gene LeBell, Morgan Roberts, Ben Rose, Will Wallace, and William Wellman Jr. for their encouragement, support, and loyal friendship.

Very special thanks to my great friend Ben McCain for sharing his powerful and heartfelt story in the foreword to this book. Ben is a multi-talented actor, author, producer, director, singer, songwriter, and host with a wealth of wisdom to share with young actors. You can find his picture in the dictionary next to the word "friend."

Introduction

Thank you for selecting this book. I've been in the entertainment industry for many years, but have never been an acting snob. I believe in acting as both a profession and a means of artistic expression. Though I believe in acting as a viable full-time career, I also believe in acting as an enjoyable part-time hobby or diversion. Throughout my twenty-plus years in show biz, I've seen both choices work well for performers of all sizes, shapes, ages, ethnicities, and backgrounds.

I've known some terrific actors who say they could never possibly do anything else with their lives. They eat, sleep, breathe, and dream about acting all day and all night That's all they ever talk about. I admire their one hundred percent commitment and single-minded focus.

However, I've known some equally great actors who have jobs outside of show business that they absolutely love. They are very happy with their non-industry jobs and choose to pursue acting as a fun part-time activity. They are happy with their other jobs and I'm happy for them. It's a great arrangement and helps them lead balanced lives.

I believe both the full-time and part-time options are terrific. I've heard it said that acting is not for everyone, but I disagree. Acting is for everyone. It's not just for "those special few," whoever we believe those special few to be. Stepping out into the spotlight and performing for others has a dynamic, exciting, and worldwide appeal that very few other activities can equal or recreate.

Acting on stage and screen, however, is an activity that can bring youngsters far greater benefits than just the immediate sounds of applause. The process of working on scenes and monologues every week is a wonderful way to build confidence, self-esteem, and a strong work ethic in young people. It's a proven way to help shy and introverted people become more outgoing. Acting training can also help natural extroverts – the life-of-the-party types – to become more focused, diligent, and productive as team players.

These are qualities that will serve students well in all their future endeavors. If young readers decide they'd like to pursue acting seriously as a full-time future career, it is very beneficial to begin early and give themselves every opportunity to learn as much as they possibly can. By starting young, they allow themselves to "grow up in the business." However, youngsters who ultimately decide to follow different career paths often find that the experiences they've gained from their early theatrical training proves valuable for them later in life – and in a variety of other endeavors.

Specifically, college and adult school students in engineering and the hard sciences often credit their childhood actor training for helping them develop into confident speakers and presenters. The acting skills developed in their youth make them far more comfortable in handling large-scale presentations of complex, technical material later in life – as college students and working adults. Science and engineering students are often called upon to perform technical presentations in front of large groups. Technical students with previous acting experience are at a definite advantage. Early training in performing scenes and monologues, then, is extremely valuable even for students who don't wish to pursue future careers in show business. Overall, I've observed that the benefits are powerful, substantive, and potentially life-changing.

Writing this series of monologue and scene books for young actors has been one of the most rewarding experiences of my life. I've been blessed with opportunities to work as an actor, writer, and teacher in New York, Los Angeles, and throughout the United States for more than twenty years. In that time, I've been fortunate enough to teach classes in acting, public speaking, and communications to a wide range of children, teenagers, and adult college students.

Across all age and skill levels, however, certain patterns clearly emerge. Actors of all ages and experience levels are strangely consistent in their apprehensiveness and discomfort in approaching monologues. This is true for young, beginner students, but is equally true for highly experienced adult performers.

In general, actors are not nearly as confident in performing monologues as they are in performing scenes. This is understandable, as monologues place the actor on stage all alone. I've often said that actors seem to have developed a love-hate relationship with monologues. I really wish this wasn't the case, because I've seen actors cause themselves a great deal of needless stress and frustration in rehearsing and performing monologues.

Actors love performing at a high level and knocking it out of the park for their audiences. What actors tend not to love so much is the process of selecting and practicing these new monologues. But this "behind the scenes" part of the process is even more important than the performance. Anthony Robbins, the great motivational speaker and trainer, often says that we're rewarded in public for what we practice for years in private. He's absolutely right. There is simply no substitute for preparation and training.

Selecting and rehearsing new monologues is a process actors should joyfully embrace. We should always be on the lookout for new monologues. We should seek out new material each week. We should get excited about practicing and performing new monologues and scripts. We should always be searching for new ways to stretch, expand our horizons, and become more versatile as actors. We should always try to improve our game. Human beings have a strong need to change, grow, and evolve. We all have a deep, internal desire to become the best possible versions of ourselves. It's one of the most important things we can work towards to create happy, productive, and meaningful lives.

I hope the one hundred monologues in this book will help you reach – and surpass – your goals in the performing arts and in life. Though the work is often painstaking and difficult, I can promise you that the rewards are immeasurable. Nothing worthwhile in life was ever accomplished without hard work, concentrated effort, and research.

You will find a wide variety of age-appropriate monologues in this collection. I believe if you take the time to read and study this book diligently, you'll find many different choices to fit your unique personalities, styles, and temperaments. I wish you the very best of happiness and success in all your studies and all your performances.

Always remember there's a tremendous difference between "difficult" and "impossible." If someone else has accomplished something you admire, then we know it's possible to duplicate that action – in your own unique method and style. You can accomplish the very same thing. Maybe you'll accomplish even greater things.

Stay strong, stay positive, and stay focused. You can do it. Now go get 'em.

Mike Kimmel
Los Angeles, CA

The Secret of Their Success

Everybody asks my parents the same questions. "What's your secret? What's the secret of your successful marriage? How come we never see you two fighting? How come you always look so happy together?"

But I think those are weird questions. Because to me ... that's normal. My parents always treat each other so well ... and talk to each other so nice. To me, that's just who they are. That's how they always act.

But I guess other kids' parents don't act the same. Maybe they can learn from my mom and dad. And from me ... because I'll tell you what I've observed, okay?

My mom and dad take very good care of each other. They look out for each other. They go out of their way to do stuff for each other. Little stuff ... like leaving each other friendly notes and thoughtful presents ... and taking care of things they each know the other one doesn't like to do. Mom doesn't like to clean the kitchen, so Dad does it. Dad doesn't like to go shopping, so Mom does it.

Random acts of kindness, that's what they call it.

But my dad says it best. "No man was ever shot ... while cleaning out the coffee pot."

Get Involved

Get involved, okay?

You have to be actively involved to make a difference in the world … in anything you want do with your life.

Don't wait for someone to do it for you. You have to be actively involved yourself. It's like eating a plate of delicious ham and eggs. There's a difference between that ham and those eggs. Sure, the chicken was a participant. But the pig was far more actively involved in that process.

Do you understand what I'm saying? You gotta be actively involved in the process. You gotta make a stand.

If you don't like the ham and eggs example, think about your favorite sports. How about baseball? The all-American pastime. You gotta be actively involved in a baseball game in order to help your team win. Hit, throw, field. It's all about getting involved. Every player has to do their part.

Get it? Got it? Good. Now go out there and do something. Get involved. Because nobody is interested in the won-loss record of the timekeeper, the announcer, or the referee.

Today is Tomorrow

Do you know what today is? No, I don't think you do. And I'm not talking about what you see on your calendar ... or what you see on your phone. Because today is not today at all. Today does not even resemble today.

Except right now, from where we're standing, it looks like a normal day of the week. It looks that way to the untrained eye. But that's an optical illusion. Because today is not a normal day. Today is not even today. Today is tomorrow.

Today is the tomorrow everyone talked about yesterday. Remember? We made promises to people yesterday. We made promises to ourselves. We talked about all the good things we were gonna do tomorrow. Well, tomorrow's here. Except right now, it kinda looks like ... today.

We'll study for that test tomorrow. We'll clean our room tomorrow. We'll help at home tomorrow. We'll exercise tomorrow. Well, tomorrow's here. But now we're calling it today.

So let's keep all those promises we made yesterday. All those promises about tomorrow. Because tomorrow has officially arrived, ladies and gentlemen. Today is tomorrow.

The Little Free Library

I saw the wildest thing yesterday. When I was walking home from school.

It was called The Little Free Library. That's what the sign said. Looked like a little bookcase ... except it was outside, instead of inside. In front of some people's house. I guess they put it there.

And there was a nice, friendly message taped to the inside of the glass door. It said to help yourself to a book, return it if you like, keep it if you like, and leave one for someone else if you like.

Yep, I found a book I like. And I'm gonna go back and leave one for someone else who's gonna like that one too.

And you know what I like best of all? This whole Little Free Library idea! Because people in that house paid money to build this thing just to do something nice for their neighbors – and strangers – in the community. That's being a good neighbor. And we need more good neighbors like them ... and more Little Free Libraries in every little town and big city in the world.

The Secret of Happiness

Do you know what I've observed? A lot of people are not happy. This guy on television said that eighty-three per cent of all the people in the world are not happy! Can you believe that?! Eighty-three percent!

And I don't think he was just talking about adults, either. Pretty sure kids were included in that mix.

That makes it a worldwide problem, but I think I've got the local answer. I learned it from my Aunt Grace. She's a police officer ... and she's also a single mom, so she has a pretty unique perspective ... not just on happiness, but on life in general.

She says the best way to make yourself happy is to make someone else happy too. Aunt Grace says the way to multiply happiness is to divide it. Share it with others. Because the person who needs a smile the most is the person who doesn't have one to give. And it sounds like eighty-three percent of the people out there don't have a smile to give.

So give them one of yours.

Love and Kryptonite

My big brother thought he was in love. He's in high school … so I guess he thinks he already knows everything about everything. But he doesn't know everything about dating, that's for sure. He was totally wild about this girl in his school. And they were on again, off again, on again, off again. Way too much drama if you ask me.

But nobody ever asks me! Because I'm just a kid … so I guess nobody thinks I can give them dating advice. But my brother needs some dating advice.

Because love shouldn't leave you feeling like you just got beat up. Like you just went ten rounds with Mike Tyson. Love shouldn't leave you feeling sad and tired and scared and hurt and lonely. Love is supposed to build you up, not break you down.

Love shouldn't feel like a great big chunk of kryptonite just hit you in the head … or hit you in the heart … and took all your strength away.

Love shouldn't do any of those things to you. Love should always make you feel … loved.

Love is a Verb

I'm just a kid, but I want to tell you what I know about love. Love is a verb. It's a verb. That's what gets so many people mixed up when they think about the word "love." They think love is a noun, a thing. That's why everybody's running around looking for love like it was a contact lens that rolled underneath their couch or something.

But love is a verb, not a noun. When someone says, "I love you," love is the verb in that sentence.

And a verb is an action word. So love is always active. Love is never passive. Love asks, "What can I do for you?" Love never asks, "What can you do for me?"

And when you treat it like a verb, love is not something you ever have to go looking for. When it's something you do, it comes from inside … and it's always a part of who you are. Love should always be a verb. Love should be the verb in every sentence.

Halfway Home

Sometimes, it feels like things take forever. Sometimes, it feels like we're not making any progress at all. Sometimes, it feels like nothing is happening. No forward movement. Like we're not even halfway there. Not even halfway home.

But, you know what?

Feelings are not facts. And we've gotta examine the facts. Don't base your opinion of yourself ... and any situation you're in ... on your feelings. Feelings can mess us up big time. They can wreak havoc in our lives.

Just open your book and start studying. Just go out for a run. Or even a walk. Get some exercise. Get your blood moving all around. Speak up in class and participate a little bit more. Even a little is okay. Incremental steps, right?

Just try. You can do it. Whenever you get stuck, just remember: You don't have to know the beginning, the middle, and the end. You just have to start.

Mary Shelley said, "The beginning is always today."

So let's just agree to get started. Just get yourself started. Get yourself into action and you're halfway home.

Frankenstein's Mommy

We had to read *Frankenstein* in school. For English class. Some of my classmates just wanted to watch the movie. I did too … but then I decided to kick it up a notch and read the book. And now I'm really glad I did. It's a wonderful old story.

But the most interesting part of the story, actually, was the story of the author. Mary Shelley.

Mary Shelley was only twenty-one years old. She was married to a famous author, the poet Percy Shelley. He was so famous that other famous writers used to come to their house to talk about writing … and practice their writing together.

They all decided to hold a contest to see who could write the best horror story. Guess who won? Correct! The youngest, most inexperienced writer in the group. Mary Shelley surprised them all. She wrote *Frankenstein* … and got it published too.

So, I wonder. What can you and I do … what can all of us do … even if we're the youngest, most inexperienced people in our own groups?

I think we should all find out.

Waking Up Earlier

One of my best friends in school has a little issue. Well, I think it's an issue … but my friend doesn't. My friend is always rushing. My friend is almost late almost every day for almost every appointment. My friend wakes up thirty minutes before we have to be in school. The very last minute. That's stressful. And that's just not a great way to go through life.

I think we have to get up earlier. That's what I do. I give myself plenty of time so I don't have to rush around. And get myself all nervous and stressed out like my friend does.

That just makes good, logical sense.

But good, logical sense takes time. Because logic needs a calm atmosphere to develop. Good, calm, logical sense never shows up at your door unless you make it feel welcome. And the way to do that is to get up early … so you're rested, organized, and ready for anything.

See? That just makes good, calm, logical sense.

Class dismissed.

A Four-Letter Word

I gotta say a dirty word. A four-letter word. It's a word that offends people.

Work.

It only offends people who aren't well-acquainted with it.

Work is a scary four-letter word for a whole lot of people out there. Hard work is scary times ten. But work is the secret ingredient that helps you go from where you are to where you wanna be in life. Work is the one thing that gets other things done. We can have all the best ideas and best intentions in the world, but nothing's gonna happen if we don't do something about it … and get to work.

Thomas Edison said most people miss the best opportunities that come their way because those good things show up in overalls … and look like work.

And Benjamin Franklin said that well done is always better than well said.

So … I'm sorry if I offended you. Because I'm trying to help. And, by the way, help is another four-letter word that's scary for a lot of people who don't want to become acquainted with it too.

Excuses Sound Best

Do you ever make excuses? You know, to *excuse* yourself from doing something that you really don't want to do? Sometimes we make excuses to our families. Sometimes we make excuses to our teachers. And sometimes … we even make excuses to ourselves. To *excuse* ourselves from doing our best.

I think we've all been there before. I know I have.

I couldn't do my homework because I had to watch my little brother. I didn't make the team because I didn't have the best sneakers. I didn't get the part because the director had a friend he wanted to cast instead.

But excuses don't help anything. And you know what's the worst thing about excuses? They're all valid. They're all true. They all make sense.

But we each have to decide if we're going to be an excuse-maker … or an excuse breaker. We have to ask ourselves, "Am I the kind of person who's going to make excuses … or overcome them?"

Only you can answer that question.

Because excuses always sound best to the person who's making them.

Keep Moving

Don't quit. Never stop moving forward. Forward motion is always better than standing still. That's zero motion. That's nothing. Even a rock can do that.

Remember, even if you know exactly what you want to do ... if you spend too much time thinking about doing it, you're never gonna get any part of it done. You gotta take at least one positive step forward each and every day towards that goal you have visualized in your mind.

Because even if you're on the right track, there are many tempting parking spaces along the way to distract you, convince you to rest, kick back and take a little siesta.

But think about the people we admire most. Do you think any of the people you follow ... in sports, music, acting, any other field ... stopped themselves from moving forward in life? Highly unlikely.

So don't you fall into that trap, either. Don't pull into any of those tempting parking spaces. Don't lose your focus. Don't stop to take a siesta.

You keep moving. Keep moving forward.

My Science Project

The last thing I wanted to work on this semester is the first thing that's due. My Science Fair project. How do I say this nicely? Science … and math … have never been my favorite subjects.

Nothing wrong with them … I'm just better with English, history, and drama.

So I wasn't interested in working on a science project this semester … or any semester.

But that's procrastination. And that's not helpful. So I tried to find a different approach. And apply science to something I'm interested in.

Like music. Because I play a little guitar, but I'm always trying to figure out how to increase the volume of my guitar chords. I asked my teacher if there's a science project that could help me accomplish that.

Guess what? He plays guitar too.

Guess what? He showed me how to build an old school amplifier using new school technology.

Guess what? My "Hybrid Amplifier Science Project" won second place in the Science Fair. Second place in the whole school!

Guess what? Science is my new favorite subject … but you probably guessed that part already.

Our Group Project

We're preparing for a group project in class. We're working in three-person teams, but a couple of teams are four-person. We had a couple of students left over.

Our teacher told us to break down the group project into little pieces. That way the whole thing is in bite-size chunks. You eat an elephant one bite at a time, right? So everybody has their own little part to do.

But not everybody does what they're supposed to do. Surprise, surprise. So some of those own little parts get added back into the group total. So guess who has to do them? Correct. The students who were already picked to be the team leaders – and who already have their own parts of the project to work on – have to go back and do all the work that the other team players never did in the first place.

That makes no kind of sense. The people who do nothing should try to help the team leaders.

But they don't. They're not team leaders. They're more like team leavers. I guess that's not a title, but it's definitely a thing. A minority of the people do the majority of the work. No matter how many people are in your group.

What Not To Do

I learned a valuable lesson in school today. What not to do. Knowing what not to do is equally important as knowing what to do. Sometimes, it's even more important.

Permit me to elaborate … if I may.

Have you ever heard the expression the straw that broke the camel's back? Some people are totally stressed out nowadays. Mostly grown-ups. There's days when everything goes wrong for them. If they have to deal with one more thing, it'll be way too much! More than they can handle.

Trust me. You don't want to be that one thing that pushes them over the edge. You don't wanna be that one thing that sets them off.

Because they may go off on you! They could really go nuts! And they'll blame all the other bad stuff that happened on you too. You'll be the scapegoat.

Not a good thing to be.

So learn to recognize when people are at the end of their rope. And be careful. Be careful what you say and be careful what you do. Never do anything to make people feel worse than they already do.

Cumulative

Can I ask you a question? Thank you. What's your favorite word?

Mine is "cumulative." Big word for a kid, I know. But it's a very good word ... and my favorite.

Cumulative means adding stuff up ... step by step. And each thing you add increases the total ... and builds it all up higher and higher.

In college, they talk about your cumulative grade point average ... the average of all the grades you get in all your classes. In sports, they talk about the cumulative effect of all that training and preparation we do. One thing builds upon another ... until the total is greater than the sum of its individual parts.

Many times, cumulative can describe our reputations too. Because our actions can have a cumulative effect on the way people see us. Whether we're trustworthy or not. And our daily actions build upon each other to form patterns and, eventually, habits.

So here's a cumulative idea. Build up so much cumulative good will through your positive actions and habits ... that if someone gossips about you ... if they lie about you ... or tell bad stories ... nobody would even believe it.

Little White Lies

Is it okay to tell a lie? I know most people are gonna say no, but I have friends who say it's okay sometimes. In certain situations.

Like telling a lie to protect someone. So you don't hurt their feelings. That's like doing something bad … a little bit bad … with a good intention.

Example.

Telling people they look better than they do when they really don't. Especially when they're not feeling so hot … and maybe not looking so hot.

Because that's being proactively positive and compassionate. Being a blessing in somebody's life. And that's a good thing.

I can tell by the look on your face you're not convinced. And that's okay. Because we won't agree on everything … and today we'll have to agree to disagree.

Because I've been telling some little white lies, and I'm not interested in who approves or who disapproves. She was my grandmother, not yours. And I wanted to give her something to smile about on her last few days with us.

My grandma, my choice, my little white lies, my conscience.

Third Place

My uncle was in the Olympics years ago. He doesn't talk about it much. But I saw his medal once when I was little.

It was a bronze medal ... same color as a penny, only shinier. That means my uncle came in third place. But he hardly ever talks about it. Personally, I think that's a little weird. Most people I know talk about the big, giant accomplishments of their lives all the time. A lot of people even exaggerate ... or embellish the things they've done. To make them sound bigger and more impressive.

My uncle is the opposite. He's so humble. He acts like it's no big deal. Because he thinks it really is no big deal.

"Bronze medal. That means I was only third place," my uncle says. "Two other guys did better that year. No biggie."

Okay, Uncle. Maybe two guys did better ... but that's out of all the people in the whole, wide world. Third place on our entire planet. I think that's impressive.

And I think my uncle wins first place ... the gold medal ... for being so humble and awesome.

The Santa Claus Syndrome

One of my teachers gets impatient when the class is moving too slow ... or not doing our assignments. Hate to say it, but she's actually kinda funny when she gets annoyed at us.

She asks, "What are you waiting for? Christmas?" The whole class thinks that's funny. She's just trying to tell us to stop wasting time.

And sometimes ... if the kids don't do their homework, she asks, "If you don't do it, who's gonna do it? Santa Claus?" That's funny too.

But maybe a lot of people really are waiting for Santa Claus. Maybe they don't do their homework assignments – or the stuff they have to do at home – because they're waiting for someone to do it for them. But that's being lazy.

And I'll tell you a secret. There's no Santa Claus. Santa Claus isn't coming to town. Kids gotta take responsibility for ourselves ... and not wait for people to do everything for us.

Not teachers, not parents, not classmates ... and definitely not Santa Claus.

Toy Phones

My baby sister did it again. My little baby sister played a trick on me. And I fell for it. Again. Yep. No matter how smart we think we are, every time a four-year-old hands you a toy phone … we still try to answer it.

And that's the weirdest thing of all about being a kid and growing up. We're never quite as grown-up as we think we are.

And you know what's even weirder? Grown-ups fall for that same trick too. My baby sister tricked my Uncle Charlie right after she tricked me. And Uncle Charlie's all grown up … more or less. Anyway, he's in his forties, so he should know better by now.

But Uncle Charlie still picked up my little sister's toy phone. And he started talking. Just like me, just like my big brother, just like Mom.

And just like you probably would too.

The Last Best Hope

Abraham Lincoln made this beautiful speech during the American Civil War. He made a lot of great speeches, but I did a report on this one. I found the whole speech at the library … and I thought it was beyond awesome.

President Lincoln said democracy is the last, best hope of the world. I'm sure everybody agrees … but it's weird to me that nobody wants to say it out loud. Nobody wants to verbalize it.

Like it's some kinda great big secret or something. But it's not a secret at all. Just ask people who live in countries where they don't have democracy. Countries where they have dictators and kings who can do whatever they heck they want. Those people are always trying to bring more freedom, more democratic ways of running governments into their countries. And when it doesn't work, they try to leave and find more freedom and democracy in other countries … like ours.

Those immigrants from other countries will tell you that Abraham Lincoln knew what he was talking about. Democracy really is the last, best hope of the whole, wide world.

And I'm telling everyone I know too. Starting with you.

Wanna Play a Trick?

Wanna play a trick on your friends? Here's a good one. This is a little American history quiz, and none of your friends are gonna get it right … no matter how smart they are.

Okay. Ask your friends which American President is pictured on the ten-dollar bill. Give up? No matter what answer they give you, they'll be wrong. Because Alexander Hamilton is on the ten-dollar bill … but Alexander Hamilton was never President!

Pretty sneaky, right?

Okay, here's another one. Which American President is pictured on the one hundred-dollar bill? This is a good trick if you have some rich friends. And we can all use a few of those.

Give up?

Benjamin Franklin is on the hundred-dollar bill, but Benjamin Franklin wasn't President, either.

I like these two tricks, not because I like to fool my friends, but because I like to make my friends think. And thinking is always a good thing.

And while you're thinking, think about what amazing leaders Alexander Hamilton and Benjamin Franklin must have been to have their pictures on those bills … when they weren't even President.

More Good Than Bad

A lot of people are nervous and worried. They get scared by the stuff on TV and all the bad things people tell them.

Because people who watch scary TV shows say there's werewolves, vampires, and aliens all over the place. Those bad guys are trying to get us. But people who watch more wholesome entertainment ... like family-friendly TV shows and movies ... believe something completely different. They believe blessings, miracles, and Guardian Angels are all around. Those Guardian Angels are always trying to help us.

So ... who should we believe? I guess it's up to you. People have to decide for themselves. But let me tell you what I've observed.

I think there's a lot more good than bad in this world. But sometimes we've gotta go hunting for the good ... if you know what I mean. People are basically good. There's some bad people, but there are definitely more good people than bad people. And there are more good situations, and good opportunities for people in this world ... and that's also more good than bad.

That's just my personal observation ... and I think it's a good observation ... and that's my promise to you. There's more good than bad in this world. And when we focus on the good, we create more of it. We need more good in this world. So always focus on the good.

I Was Made for More Than This

Did you ever look around and ask yourself, "How did I get into this situation?"

Why are people not treating me right? Why are things not the way they're supposed to be? Why are the kids so disrespectful in class? Why is my teacher absent so much? Why is the bus driver always late? Why is everybody looking at their phones when they're talking to me?

How come everything's not right? Why is there so much laziness and disrespect? I was made for more than this.

I was not meant to swim around in this rude little guppy pool. Where everybody underperforms. I was meant for bigger and better things. But in order to do bigger and better things, you have to become bigger and better yourself.

You have to become a new type of person on this Earth. There's only one of you, and you have to be the best possible version of that one person.

And seeing all this disrespect .... makes me want to act better. Because I know for a fact ... I was made for more than this.

I Forgot What I Like

Did you ever forget what you like?

I went to that fancy coffee place with my mom. I don't drink coffee … my mom drinks coffee, but she picked me up after school and that's where she wanted to go.

We've been there before. And they have a bunch of non-coffee drinks there for the kids. Some are like big, giant milk shakes. Some are more like smoothies. Some are like chocolate milk.

They're all different and they're all good. And … that's kinda the problem. That one's a good one. That one's a good one. And that one's a really good one.

How can I choose the best among all those good choices? Maybe they're all good, but I liked that one yesterday, I liked the green smoothie one last week, and I liked the big milk shakey one the time before that.

How can I choose? I liked that one best yesterday, but today it's only second best … not much better than the rest.

This is embarrassing, but … I think I forgot what I like.

They Speak Perfect English!

I like movies, I really do. But there's some things in the movies that kinda bug me.

Did you ever notice that Foreign Military Officers ... whenever they speak to each other alone ... they always speak English? What's that all about?

Even aliens from outer space. When you see those superhero movies, every time a bad guy comes down to Earth, they always speak English!

Okay, okay, maybe they're advanced enough to have an electronic language translator. I could see that.

But even when our favorite superheroes run into bad guy aliens in outer space ... those aliens always speak perfect English too!! I guess they have a lot of English teachers ... and grammar textbooks floating around up there in outer space.

Okay, now that I got that off my chest ... there's one more thing that bothers me in the movies.

Back here on Planet Earth – did you ever notice that every single woman in a movie ... every lady who's not married ... always has a cat? What's up with that? What's wrong with dogs? Why do single ladies in the movies always have to have a cat?

How Much is Too Much?

I saw this guy at the mall. The wildest looking guy. All covered with tattoos. On his face too. More tattoos than I ever saw.

He had so many tattoos, there wasn't any more room on him. I don't think there were any blank skin spaces left. If he wanted another tattoo, I'm not sure he could get one printed.

So I asked myself … how does someone know when to stop? Stop getting tattoos, I mean.

Because I've seen a whole lot of people with a whole lot of tattoos. But this man gets the prize. The Most Tattoos Award. The Blue Ribbon for Most Tattoos.

And I understand. After you get a whole lot of something … you want to get a whole lot more. To keep that momentum going. Like collecting baseball cards. Or comic books.

But how much is too much? Too many, I mean. Because tattoos are countable items, not uncountable items.

And I don't have the answer. I don't think this man at the mall does, either. But maybe he should … because they're his tattoos.

The Mighty Mustache Men

I saw a man on TV with a funny mustache. I never saw a mustache like that before. It went up instead of down. With a little Curly-Q too. It was so funny.

My father liked it too. Dad used to have a mustache, but he shaved it off. He said he could never keep it straight and even. Sometimes, one side grew too long, and he cut it to match the shorter side. Then the shorter side would be too long and it wasn't even again.

Also, Dad said whenever he ate soup, the smell of his soup would stay in his mustache all day long.

That's a lot of maintenance. I guess mustaches can be too much work for some men.

But not all men.

That guy on TV doesn't think it's too much work. Somehow, he figured it out. And maybe that's not right for everybody. But for any man on this planet who wants to grow and maintain a mustache – especially a big, funny, Curly-Q mustache – the evidence proves that it's certainly achievable.

Mike Kimmel

The Karaoke Man

My Uncle Johnny is going to his second job tonight. He calls that moonlighting. I don't think anybody uses that expression anymore. They used it back in the day from what I understand. Uncle Johnny always talks about the good old days.

But he calls these the good new days. And Uncle Johnny goes to his second job on Friday and Saturday nights with the same attitude he always has ... an excellent one.

My uncle played music with bands when he was younger. He wasn't famous, but he made a lot of money as a studio musician. Studio musicians play background music for the famous musicians when they're recording songs. He was an excellent one.

I'm sure he would like to still be making big money like he made years ago. But he's not. Nowadays, Uncle Johnny sets up the karaoke machine at a restaurant on Friday night ... and a different one on Saturday night. He sings with the people. He laughs and tells jokes.

They don't pay him too much ... and there's only a few people in the audience ... but nobody would know that from my Uncle Johnny's attitude ... which is always the same ... an excellent one.

Do You Need Anything?

D o you need anything?"

That's what my Uncle Carmine always asks me. Every single time he sees me, he asks me the same question. "Do you need anything?" And not just me. That's what he asks everybody. Every single person. Uncle Carmine's always doing something nice for somebody ... even for people he doesn't know.

Bringing people food. Giving them money. Fixing their cars. Driving them to the airport. Whatever somebody might need, Uncle Carmine does it. Why? I don't know. I guess he just wants to do good things here in the world.

That's a totally different motivation than most people you see running around down here on Planet Earth.

And I think it's a good motivation. And that's what I wanna do too.

So ... how about you? How are you today? Are you all right? What can I do for you? I can't drive you to the airport, but I can do some other stuff. I can help you with your homework. I can teach you how to ride a bike. I can share my sandwich. I can give you a cookie.

Do you need anything?

The Encyclopedia of Cupcakes

I just celebrated my birthday. It was on the sixteenth. Someone asked me what year. I told them, "Every year." Hey, nobody needs to know my personal information.

But you know what another birthday means, right? Time for a special surprise. No, no, no. Not just a gift … although those are nice too.

Even better are my mom's special cupcakes she bakes for all of our birthdays. My sister's birthday and mine. They're better than a birthday cake. Exponentially better … by like a factor of a thousand.

They're so good – you could say my mom practically wrote the book on cupcakes. Actually, she could write a whole encyclopedia. The Encyclopedia of Cupcakes.

And my mom's kinda like that, you know? She does lots of things better than anyone else. Exponentially better. I don't know how she does all she does – but I'm really glad she does.

I'm really glad she's my mom, too. Cupcakes or no cupcakes.

Strong Coffee

Two words. Strong coffee.

That's my father's secret identity. Strong coffee turns him into the world's greatest superhero. Gives him tons of energy.

My father works two jobs and goes to school at night. My mother says he's burning the candle at both ends. I never really heard that expression before, but I understand it because it's visual. You can see a picture in your mind. And that picture looks exactly like my father. Describes him perfectly. Because he's always rushing from one thing to the next.

That's why he depends upon strong coffee. He say it's like his super-charged octane fuel that helps him get through the day.

Mom said he shouldn't just try to "get through the day." My mother always tells my father to slow down and enjoy the day.

This morning she said, "Stop and smell the roses." Dad got real excited. He thought that was great.

Dad said, "Good idea! That's what we need. I'm gonna go buy some rosebushes. I'm gonna plant us some roses. That's my weekend project."

Yep. That's some strong coffee my father drinks.

Chewing Gum in Class

My teacher is starting to get tough on us. With all the students in my class. She's really starting to crack down. Especially on all those little, itty-bitty rules the kids in my class try to break.

Especially the stupidest rule in our school. No chewing gum allowed. Hello!

Why is this even an issue anymore? With my classmates, I mean. All the kids in my class should know this already. We've known it since we were little and itty bitty ourselves.

No chewing gum in class. It's rude. It's disrespectful. It's loud. It's messy. It's obnoxious. And it's against the rules. Duh! Is this hard to figure out or something?

Not really. It's just that the kids in my class have gotten sloppy with the rules. Which is kinda why our teacher is cracking down now … and why I'm telling you this in the first place.

No chewing gum in class. Period. End of story. That's the rule. Make sure it sticks with you. Get it? Sticks with you. Like chewing gum. Get it? Got it? Good.

We Got a New Teacher

We got a new teacher in my class. Our regular teacher had to leave in the middle of the semester. Personal problems of some kind.

We didn't exactly find out all the details ... but we knew it must be something serious. Because our teacher loved her job ... and would never have left if she didn't have to.

So it was a little hard for our class to accept a new teacher. We didn't want this new teacher. We didn't want any new teacher. Didn't matter who it was gonna be ... no matter how good, how smart, and how qualified ... we just wanted our regular teacher back.

Do you see where I'm going with this? Good, because it's a little embarrassing.

The new teacher assigned to our class was not welcome at all. And we showed it too. Nobody participated in class, nobody did their homework, and everybody misbehaved ... we never respected the new teacher like we respected our old teacher.

I guess we made her job pretty difficult. And we won't get a chance to apologize, either. Because the principal just came in and told us that she quit and she's never coming back to our school again.

We got a new teacher in my class. And now we lost her ... just like we lost our old teacher.

The Good Morning Experiment

My Uncle Charlie is conducting an experiment. Not in a science lab ... in the real world ... the laboratory of life.

Uncle Charlie is the friendliest grown-up I know. Much friendlier than my teachers or any of my parents' friends.

Uncle Charlie says ... "Good Morning." He says, "Good Morning" to everyone he sees ... everyone in the whole, wide world. That's my Uncle Charlie. Told you he was friendly.

And it's not just "Good Morning," by the way. He gives people a great big wave and an even bigger smile. Flashing those pearly whites.

But the responses he gets are kind of amazing! All different! All over the map! That's the purpose of his study. Some people wave back. Some people give him a little bitty fake smile. And some people just ignore him completely. That last category was a big surprise!

Try this yourself. Conduct your own Good Morning experiment. Be as nice and as friendly as you can be tomorrow morning. And every following morning. Give a great big, happy "Good Morning" to every person you meet. Flash those pearly whites ... and see what happens. Your results ... your own scientific data ... may surprise you too.

The Homework Compartment

I have a friend who always asks me to help with homework. Well, we definitely get too much homework, but … I'm not so sure this kid is too much of a friend.

This kid texts me, emails me all the time. Invites me to the house to help with homework and studying for tests. What do you think of my writing? How's my grammar? What's a good topic for an essay?

And I'm always available to help. That's what friends are for. I don't mind. But then I noticed … my friend posts all this other stuff … about pizza parties … video games … cool stuff, fun stuff … but I never get invited to any of those things. I only get invited to help with homework.

What the heck is that all about? I like pizza parties and video games too. Not just homework. Doesn't exactly make me feel very … appreciated.

Nobody likes to be compartmentalized. If you're my friend … then be my friend one hundred per cent … in all compartments and all departments.

Don't just invite me into the homework compartment of your life.

Your Next Right Move

We have choices. We have options. That's indisputable. It's irrefutable. This is not up for debate. A hundred times a day, we can turn left or we can turn right.

Daily decisions. We all have decisions to make daily. Sometimes those are little decisions. But that doesn't make them meaningless decisions.

A lot of people don't like to make decisions. Maybe they don't like the responsibility. But not making a decision is also making a decision … because then we're making a decision to do nothing … and just let things happen to us.

And that's not exactly the best strategy. It's like a pilot getting into the airplane and not deciding where to go. Can you imagine that? The plane can't get to its destination if that pilot doesn't think about which direction to go. That's the pilot's next right move.

And we all have to make our next right move. Sometimes we're waiting for other people to tell us what to do. But so many things are really up to us. Even making little decisions is important. That's good practice for us every day. That helps us prepare to make those bigger decisions when we have to.

Two Wolves

I spend a lot of time with my grandfather. I think he's the smartest person I've ever seen. Actually, I think he's the smartest person anyone's ever seen.

Grandpa told me a story about two wolves. He said there are two wolves fighting inside of us at all times. Not just me and him, but all of us.

We all have two wolves. One wolf is wild and dangerous. He's always prowling around, looking for someone to attack. Because that wolf is filled with rage, hate, jealousy, un-forgiveness, dishonesty, selfishness, and fear.

Meanwhile, the other wolf is calm, strong, and confident. This wolf is filled with love, joy, contentment, happiness, truth, and peace. He never attacks anybody … but he knows he can defend himself whenever he needs to.

Grandpa said those two wolves fight each other forever. There's a fight going on every day inside of us. There's a fight every day between two wolves inside our minds. They fight for control of our lives.

So I asked my grandfather which wolf wins the fight. Grandpa said the winner is always the stronger wolf … it's the wolf you decide to feed every day.

Train Your Brain

The world is filled with talented people. Unfortunately, many talented people never do anything. They never accomplish their goals. Why is that?

Our bodies have limitations. Our minds do not. So many talented people have goals, but never reach those goals ... they never even get anywhere near them. Goals are like New Year's resolutions for a lot of people. They make New Year's resolutions every January and forget about them by February!

A lot of talented people never approach their resolutions, never get near their big, major goals. And they never get anywhere near figuring out where their limitations are, either. That's the trick.

Because our minds don't have limitations like our bodies do. That's why athletes can only last so long. They can't play baseball and football forever. But they can train their brains to do a whole lot more than they ever could do when they were in the best shape of their lives playing sports.

People test their bodies all day long. But try to test the limits of your mind with me instead. Train your brain. You'll find it's quite a test ... because your mind is quite limitless.

Don't Shrink Yourself

I put my favorite T-shirt in the laundry and got the settings all wrong. It shrunk so much I can't even wear it now. Maybe I can still use it for a bandana.

That was a mistake. My fault. But, you know what … a lot of people do that same thing on purpose. Not with their clothes, but with their lives. They shrink themselves down to fit into smaller places, with smaller responsibilities, and smaller opportunities.

Deep down, a lot of people know they can do better. They can, but they won't. Maybe they don't want to show off. Maybe they don't want to intimidate those around them. Maybe they're afraid people will feel bad.

But what about you? You're a people.

A person, I mean. And you owe it to yourself to make the most of what nature gave you to work with.

If you know you can do better … then start doing better. Don't shrink yourself down to fit into places you've already outgrown.

I'm Tough on Myself

I'm tough on myself. People say I shouldn't be. But I want to do well. I want to be my best.

One of my teachers said that makes me a perfectionist. And that's not good. But I don't agree.

I'm not a perfectionist. I'm a possibilitist. I don't think that's a real word, but I know you'll forgive me for that. Because I know I'll never be perfect. Because nobody gets to be perfect. Even perfectionists.

I know that even Muhammad Ali lost a few fights. Even Michael Jordan missed a few shots. But they didn't give up or get discouraged. They kept going.

And that's what I do. I keep going because I'm a possibilitist. So even if I don't get a good grade on a test … even if I mess up in sports … I believe in all possibilities.

Including the possibility of getting just a little bit better day by day.

And that's why I'm tough on myself. I'm tough on myself to help me get better. I'm tough on myself so other people don't have to be.

The Distraction Attraction

Do you ever get distracted? Me too. I used to get distracted all the time ... especially when I had something important to do. Like studying for a big test. Trying out for sports. Or ... just last year when I promised to help my little sister learn to read.

Those are very important things to do. Extremely important. Much more important than the insignificant little things that kept me from doing my best. And kept me from keeping my word.

Like playing video games ... watching cartoons ... or wasting way too much time on my phone. I don't even know why I do stuff like that. Maybe you can relate.

It's a distraction. There's a distraction attraction. I know there is. And distraction leads to procrastination. So ... why do I keep going back to those same meaningless distractions again and again and again?

I don't know. I'm young, but I've been dealing with a distraction attraction all my life. I can't find anything good about it, either. If there was some kinda benefit to distraction and procrastination .... I probably would have found it by now.

Choices and Decisions

Life is all about choices and decisions. You can make a positive choice or you can make a negative choice.

You can show up with a good attitude. You can show up with a bad attitude. With your family, friends ... school, sports, everywhere. It's your choice.

I learned that from my Uncle Mickey. My friendly, good-natured Uncle Mickey.

Uncle Mickey was sad and gloomy for a long, long time. My uncle had a lot of bad things happen in his life. He explained to me that he had to make a decision. Do we live in a friendly world or do we live in an unfriendly world? That's a choice and decision we can make every day.

Uncle Mickey chose to live in a friendly world. He decided he wanted to do his best to make our world a little friendlier every day ... as much as one person possibly can.

We can all do the same thing. Decide today to multiply the good. You can make a positive decision. You can make a negative decision.

It's your choice every day. Choose wisely.

The Danger of Anger

Don't get mad. And if you're already mad, then try not to stay mad. A wise man said anger is fundamentally self-defeating. That means it can beat us up from the inside out – even when it feels like nothing in the outside world can ever beat us.

Anger is one letter away from danger. Anger is very closely aligned with danger. All you have to do is slap a "d" on the front of your "anger" and it becomes "danger." And the "d" also stands for "dumb," because that's what I think anger really is. It's just plain dumb.

But don't listen to me. I'm just a kid. Listen to Epictetus … he was a famous philosopher from thousands of years ago. Difficult name, though. I don't know why his parents couldn't have just named him Johnny. But Epictetus asked, "Why should we get angry at the world? As if the world would notice."

I think he's right. Epictetus was a smart man. It's a great lesson for us all. So I'm never gonna get angry again.

I won't even get angry with that philosopher's parents for naming him Epictetus.

A Drinking Problem. A Drinking Solution.

My uncle had a drinking problem for years. He finally gave it up. He said one day he got to the point where he was almost going to do something bad … with some friends who also had a drinking problem. And he just didn't wanna go there.

So he finally turned his life around. Funny how so many people can still turn their lives around and do something better … even after a long time making mistakes.

It's sad to see people with that problem. But it's good to know it's never too late to make a better decision … and turn your life around.

After my uncle stopped drinking, he stopped smoking too. Said he felt like he was on a roll. Really making progress … and he felt motivated to keep going.

Nowadays, you wouldn't recognize my uncle. He exercises, eats healthy, and even stopped using bad words. He says he feels better than he has in years. Looks great too. Says he's drinking from the fountain of youth now. Drinking deeply from the well of life.

And that's the kind of drinking that's more of a solution than a problem.

The Monkey-Chicken

You know what kids in my school always talk about? Bullying. That conversation is everywhere. We all know this is a big problem nowadays.

But bullying is nothing new. It's been around forever. It's older than rope. My father got bullied when he was my age. The other kids said horrible stuff. They teased him all the time. They called him "Monkey-Chicken." They said he talked like a monkey and walked like a chicken. If a monkey and a chicken had a kid, it would look just like him.

Monkey-Chicken! Craziest put-down ever!

Well, my dad could handle it. He said, "Good! That means I'm special. I'm the only Monkey-Chicken on this planet. The circus can hire me, take me all over the world, and I'll be famous. I'll make millions of dollars. I'll be on TV. And I'll be the very best Monkey-Chicken anyone could ever imagine!"

I love my father's attitude. That's how I wanna be. When someone's mean to me, I remember the simplest rule. "Sticks and stones can break my bones, but names can never hurt me."

Not even a name as stupid as "Monkey-Chicken."

The Great Encourager

You should meet my Uncle Johnny. We call him the Great Encourager. Funny nickname, right? But what he does is not funny at all. It's actually really serious and really great.

He encourages everybody. He encourages family, close friends ... and even strangers who he just met. The first time he meets people, he always says something uplifting, optimistic ... something to make sure he can help someone have a better day than they were having – before he ever popped into their lives with that good word. That's a gift that he gives to people all day long. I don't know how he does it.

But I think everybody needs a Great Encourager in their life. Even ... a "Not So Great Encourager." A "Pretty Good Encourager" may be enough ... or even a "So-So Encourager." That's still a good place to start.

You gotta start somewhere. You'll get better with practice.

I'm starting today. I wanna encourage people.

Wanna join me? Come on. Don't be afraid. Don't be embarrassed. I'm encouraging you to join me.

I'm an Encourager

I'm an encourager. I always tell my friends, family, my classmates that they're doing great. I always try to encourage people. That's what an encourager does. People ask me why I'm so happy. Why I'm in a good mood all the time. How can I always stay so positive?

You wanna know the reason?

Because of my ears. What does that mean? It means when I speak out a positive message ... or say something encouraging to another person, I noticed something super interesting. I can make someone else feel better ... but I feel better too.

That's because my own ears are so close to my mouth. In fact, they're the closest ears in the world to my mouth. So my ears hear those encouraging words, those positive thoughts, before anybody else's.

Who knows? Maybe that means I benefit from those positive messages even more than the people I'm telling them to.

And that's why I'm an encourager. I think we should all be encouragers. Because I'm positive proof. We all benefit from the positive messages we give to other people. Our own ears are the first ones to hear them.

A Moth: Tiny and Mighty

We were getting ready for a long trip. Dad rolled the windows down to air out the car while we packed our stuff.

Then I saw the strangest thing. A little grey moth flew in the driver's side window.

He was buzzing around, buzzing around inside our car ... trying to find his way out. He looked stressed ... lost, hopeless ... but he kept bopping around, bopping around, side to side ... trying to find his way back out.

So weird. I couldn't take my eyes off this little guy. I felt so bad for him. He was lost.

Why couldn't he find the same window he flew in to fly out? I don't know, but he clearly needed help. So I reached out, opened the door, and out he went.

But I wonder why he couldn't find his way back by himself. Kinda like my Uncle Charlie. A little lost. I think a lot of people are like that little lost moth. A lot of people need someone to look after them. A lot of people just need someone to help them out a little bit.

People need someone to open a door for them once in a while. Maybe even more than once in a while. There's a lot of little lost moths out there.

Open Doors

Sometimes in life, you feel like nothing's working. Like nothing good is happening for you.

But things are always happening when we're not watching and expecting them. Just because it looks like nothing is happening right now, there could be a lot happening that was already started ... already set in motion ... a long time ago.

For example, we had ... not the greatest teacher last year. None of the kids in my class were learning too much. Then, all of a sudden ... they transferred that teacher to a new school and we got a brand-new teacher that's so much better.

And the same thing happened with my mother's job. She wanted to look for something different. It wasn't too good for her. Then ... all of a sudden, they gave her a different job at the same place. And she likes her new job much better than the old one.

These are good examples. Sometimes it looks like a door is closed for you ... but that's because you're looking at it from the inside.

Meanwhile, on the outside ... someone's getting ready to open that door. With a nice, new surprise that will be just perfect for you.

Ornithology

Ornithology.

My uncle Richard calls that a five-dollar word ... a really big word, he means.

Ornithology is the study of birds. But you probably knew that already. Uncle Richard is an ornithologist, a bird watcher. He says we should all spend more time watching birds. Because when we're watching birds, we're looking up, not down. That makes it much easier to see all the beautiful rainbows in your life. Pretty smart, right?

Uncle Richard has a million books on ornithology. He took me with him on a bird-watching expedition yesterday. He pointed out all the different kinds of birds. He explained the differences between them. He took notes and drew pictures in the little bird watching notebook he carries around. He bought me a little bird watching notebook too.

Honestly, I never noticed all those different birds. But you know what I did notice? The whole time I was out there bird-watching, I never once looked at my phone.

I'm not sure if ornithology is exactly right for me, but I think everyone should do something every day ... that makes us forget to check our phones.

Bird on a Branch

I was sitting in class, but I was distracted. I was looking out the window at a beautiful little bird in a tree. Sitting there all by itself and singing.

A little bird sitting on a tree branch is never afraid of falling. Never afraid of the branch breaking. Because that bird is not placing its trust on that branch. It's placing its trust on its own two wings. That bird is filled with self-confidence. A little, tiny bird that probably doesn't even weigh one pound ... but that bird believes in itself.

What about us? We're bigger, stronger, more intelligent than any bird. Our brains are a million times more developed. So why do we waste so much time worrying about our own tree branches ... all those things that support us and keep us upright?

We can learn a lot from a little bird ... and how that little bird knows to trust itself. Maybe we can learn to stop doubting ourselves ... and begin to see ourselves the way birds see themselves.

Strong, confident, free ... and capable of soaring to unimaginable heights.

Rose Bushes

Abraham Lincoln said we can complain because rose bushes have thorns or rejoice because thorn bushes have roses.

Many people say Lincoln was America's greatest President. Maybe he was, but you know what he got?

Shot is what he got. Lincoln was assassinated. Which means that even if you're a great person and doing all kinds of good things with your life, there's going to be somebody who doesn't like you.

My Grandma Mollie says you can be the nicest, sweetest, most beautiful apple in the entire orchard ... and there's still gonna be someone who doesn't like apples.

Not everybody is going to like you, and not everybody is going to appreciate what you have to offer, That's a good lesson to remember. So do your best to maintain a sense of perspective.

We can't do anything about the way people treat us, but we can train ourselves to avoid thorny situations in life ... as much as possible, anyway.

And that frees us up to find all those roses that are waiting to share their unique beauty and fragrance with us. I promise you, the roses are always there for you.

And the roses are always worth the thorns.

I'm a Collector

I'm a collector. I collect something very valuable. No, not stamps, coins, comic books, or Pokemon cards. Do they still make Pokemon cards? They probably do. But I collect something even better.

I collect quotes. Famous quotations from brilliant men and women of the past. I save them on my phone. I also save them in a little notebook.

I have quotes from all kinds of people – writers, actors, artists, musicians, historians, and politicians. Those quotes help me when I'm having … kind of a rough day.

Example. Elvis Presley said, "When things go wrong, don't go with them."

That's one of my favorites.

And when I don't know what to do, I remember Theodore Roosevelt's words of wisdom. "Do what you can, with what you have, where you are."

When I'm not feeling too confident, I go back to what Marilyn Monroe said. "We are all of us stars, and we deserve to twinkle."

Sometimes it's hard being a kid … trying to figure everything out. But, with my quote collection, I don't have to figure everything out by myself. I have help from all those beautiful, brilliant thinkers from all those years ago.

Horrible Cookies. Beautiful Container.

I ate the most horrible cookies yesterday. The absolute, worst cookies I ever had in my whole, entire life. My mother bought them at my favorite store, but these are no way my favorite cookies.

My mom said she doesn't like 'em either, but she likes the box. Wants to use it for her craft projects. I think it's kinda weird to buy something you don't like and then have to eat it … just to get a box to keep something else in.

I started thinking. Maybe a lot of people are like that too. Beautiful container on the outside, but … maybe they're not quite so nice on the inside. Maybe a little less than savory. Maybe even horrible.

Yeah, yeah, I know. Don't overthink. But there's a valuable lesson to be learned about people here, I promise.

Because those horrible cookies really left a bad taste in my mouth.

My Fictitious Big Brother

My big sister's doing something weird. I'm just a kid, but I don't agree with what she's doing. Of course, she's in high school, so you know how that goes.

My big sister created a fictitious big brother for herself. Therefore, he's a fictitious big brother for me too! But this is not right.

Whenever she gets in trouble at school … late with a homework assignment … skips a class … fails a test because she didn't study … who does she blame?

You guessed it – our fictitious big brother, Jeff. She even gave him a name.

Jeff gets our family into all kinds of trouble. Someone always has to rescue him. Last week, Jeff smacked up his motorcycle. Before that, Jeff got kicked out of college. Before that, Jeff had some other major drama.

Jeff is a great big mess. Most fictitious people are. So he's a convenient scapegoat for every mistake my sister makes.

Look, I'm just a kid, but I think this is wrong. And I don't want any of their bad behavior – fictitious or otherwise – rubbing off on me.

Don't Use ALL CAPS!

I can't believe some people. Like my friend Alex.

Well ... I thought Alex was my friend. Until this morning. But now I'm going to have to reconsider that relationship. Because Alex just texted me in all caps! ALL CAPS!

That is so rude. Rude times ten. Nobody should use all caps. Ever! Unless you're mad at somebody. Because ALL CAPS makes it look like you're yelling at them. And that's definitely not cool. Completely disrespectful. Might even qualify as a micro-aggression. It probably is ... because there's so many micro-aggressions out there already these days. So who the heck needs one more?!

Not me. That's for sure.

Alex was way out of line, and I'm not gonna stand for it. No. Don't try to talk me out of it, either. I've made up my mind. Alex is officially out. I'm unfriending Alex.

I'm sending out the notice today ... on all social media platforms. And I'm spelling it in all lowercase letters ... so nobody thinks it's disrespectful.

The Dentist's Office

I went to the dentist with my dad. Not for me, for him. He's the patient this time. Dad just asked me to go with him for moral support. That's funny, right?

My dad goes to the gym four times a week. My dad can lift three hundred pounds. But my dad's afraid to go to the dentist by himself.

I get it. Just because you're strong in one area doesn't mean you're strong in another. And the hard thing about being the strongest person is that nobody ever asks you if you need help. This is one area where my dad definitely needs help. That's where I come in. Dad doesn't say he's scared to go to the dentist, but I can tell.

And I can help.

I sit in the waiting room with my father and keep him company. I talk to him about other stuff to distract him. I remind him that everything's gonna be all right.

Then I remind him of all the times he showed me that everything's gonna be all right too. And I calm him down until he believes me.

World Champion Style

Something wild happened. I met my uncle's friend from college. They were roommates. Played sports together too.

This guy was really good at sports. After graduation, he even set a world record. He was interviewed for magazines and TV. Even got his name in the Guinness Book of World Records. Naturally ... because he ... set a world record.

My uncle invited him for dinner. We heard stories about him for years. He looked amazing, still in great shape. I guess he never stopped exercising. That's unusual. My uncle's other friends slowed down as they got older. They got heavy too. This guy looked like he could still set world records.

That's impressive. But what I liked best about my uncle's friend were his good manners. And how calm and friendly and polite he was. He acted so nice to everybody at dinner. Someone asked about that, and he said it's something he learned from setting his world record.

He said that since breaking the world record, he wanted to try and do everything in his life that same way ... the best way he possibly could. ... like he's imagining that he's going for the world record in everything he does.

World champion style.

She's So Good

My Aunt Susie was in a movie when she was younger. She's a really good actress. She's so good.

She was my first acting coach. She teaches adults, but started a class for younger people when she heard I was interested. Susie told my mom I could be in her class for free for as long as I want. Even forever.

My Aunt Susie's pretty awesome. Guess you figured that out already.

Her movie was on TV last night. We stayed up late to watch. She was so good. Probably the best actor in that movie. So I'm surprised she didn't do more movies. She mostly teaches acting classes now. That's her main job. She's getting older now too, but I know she could have been a big star. She's so good.

Some actors who should be famous actors never get to be famous actors … and I don't understand why. But … you know how many times I've heard my Aunt Susie complain about that? Zero. She never complains.

My Aunt Susie's very humble. Says she's happy teaching her students everything her teachers taught her years ago. She always says she likes to give something back. I believe her too.

She's so good.

I Always Ask Questions

I always ask questions. Because questions help us get real facts and understand the world.

Example. My mother goes to church and reads the Bible, but my father doesn't. My mother says we all descended from Adam and Eve. My father says we all descended from monkeys.

That's a big difference in opinion. Polar opposites. Not too much room for compromise.

Who's right? Where did we all come from?

Is my mom right? Did we come from Adam and Eve? Then where is the Garden of Eden?

Is my dad right? Did we come from monkeys? Then why do we still have monkeys running around on this planet? How come they're not extinct?

I don't have those answers, because I think these are the big questions people have been asking for hundreds of years.

But I noticed that my parents are always so very respectful to each other – even though they disagree on important questions. So the real question is … why can't all married couples treat each other as nice as my parents do?

And that's a very important question to ask.

The Marshmallow Test

The Marshmallow Test.

A professor in a big university did an experiment with kids my age. It's a famous experiment now, and they call it The Marshmallow Test.

They told kids they could have a marshmallow. They gave each kid one marshmallow. But if kids could wait a few minutes, they could have two marshmallows instead.

Then the professor leaves the room and comes back in fifteen minutes. The kids who didn't eat the marshmallow ... got a second marshmallow for a reward. But the kids who ate their first marshmallow got a great big box of nothing.

What was the purpose? They watched those kids years later and found out that the kids who waited fifteen minutes to eat their marshmallow did better in school and better at work.

They call it a self-control experiment. If you can resist an immediate temptation in front of you ... and wait for a better reward, then that shows good study habits, good work habits, and good character.

What about you? Are you a one marshmallow or a two marshmallow kind of person? It's something sweet to think about, for sure.

Be Careful What You Talk About

Do grown-ups tell you to be careful? Good. They're trying to help. Because grown-ups get kinda nervous about us kids.

And they should be nervous. Because a lot of people do something dangerous out there in the world. Wanna guess what it is? Talking without thinking. Very dangerous. We gotta watch our words. Yeah, words. We gotta be careful speaking about what we're speaking about. Because words have power. So it's important to mostly talk about good things ... and all the things you want to do, and have, and be in your life.

That sends good messages out of our mouths and into our minds. It helps us be happy and do good, productive things all day long. But if we speak out something negative, it can have a negative effect.

Example. Never say, "This math chapter is so hard. I'll never understand it." Instead, you can say, "This is hard, but I'm a pretty smart kid. I can learn it if I keep trying. I learned plenty of hard stuff before, and I can study and learn this too."

Get the idea? Don't talk about the difficult problem. Talk about the solution you're figuring out. Little by little. Step by step. Because words have power. So learn to use that power as well as you can for your own good. Talk about what you want, not what you don't want.

Class dismissed.

How Old Should I Be?

Maybe you can help me. I'm trying to figure out the best age for a person to be.

I wish that was my exact age right now. Apparently that's not the case. Because my mom and dad always say I'm too young. Sometimes they say it differently. I'm too little.

"You can stay up late when you get older." "You can walk the dog when you get bigger." "You can ride the bus by yourself … uh … in a few more years."

But how many years will make me my perfect age? And then … how many more years … before I get too old?

Because Grandpa's not an ideal age, either. He's always saying he's too old to stay up late. Too old to walk the dog. And – man, oh man – he hasn't taken the bus in years. So what's the perfect age? Because I'm too young and my grandfather is too old.

Maybe somewhere in the middle? Like Goldilocks. Not too hot, not too cold. Not too young, not too old. Just right. I wonder how old Goldilocks was when she became famous … for trespassing, breaking and entering, and burglary.

Don't look at me like that, okay? You know she didn't pay for that porridge. Yeah, yeah, yeah … I know what you're thinking.

What the heck is porridge?

Building That Car

My dad loves cars. He grew up very poor. His parents didn't have a car when he was a kid.

He was always interested in cars since he was little ... even though his family didn't have one for him to ride in ... and learn in.

But he had a little plastic model car that he built. You know, one of those plastic ones from the hobby shop that you glue together and then paint.

A Ford Mustang. That was his favorite. Then, when he was a teenager, and started working at a couple of part-time jobs after school, Dad saved his money. Little by little, he bought parts of old Ford Mustang cars from junkyards and garage sales.

He read car magazines and learned as much about them as he could. He was so interested, he learned how to build a car. From all the little parts he collected.

It took a long time, but my father did it. And now, we have a real car in our driveway just like the little plastic one he made when he was a kid.

And my father built both of them. The little bitty plastic one and the big, shiny metal one. Because every dream you dream can someday become real.

The Beautiful Blue Car

My father drives a beautiful blue car. It's fourteen years old, but it still runs pretty well. A little noisy. And it's got a few scratches. Well ... more than a few scratches. Guess it doesn't ride as smooth as my uncle's car does. Doesn't take bumps and pot-holes too well. The window on the passenger side doesn't open. And sometimes the air conditioning doesn't get cold enough.

So I guess it's not exactly perfect. But my dad just LOVES his beautiful blue car. He says one of these days he's gonna clean it up nice and shiny ... and put it in a big auto show ... for the whole world to see it – and enjoy it – as much as he does.

Because he's so proud of that car. He appreciates it so much. Even though it's not exactly perfect, Dad says it's perfect for him. Dad says that car represents freedom to go anywhere. Opportunity to work and make a living. Peace of mind to take us out to dinner anytime we want.

Because the car itself is neutral. The car's just an object ... not positive, not negative. What's important is our attitude to-wards that object. And my dad's attitude is really something to see. It's truly amazing.

So maybe we'll take you for a ride sometime. Because you should see that beautiful blue car rolling on down the road. And you should see my beautiful true-blue dad ... so happy, so proud, and so grateful behind the wheel.

The Mission

I was watching this guy on TV. Totally inspiring ... and actually kinda philosophical, too. He was talking ... to adults, mostly ... about why we're here. On Planet Earth, I mean.

And he wasn't just talking about people's jobs, either. He said human beings are made for more than just the earthly things we spend our time and money on.

He was talking about our greater purpose in life. Not our passion. Not what we're passionate about doing. That's just our personal interest inventory.

Our higher purpose in life, though, is a little bit different. It's what we're meant to be doing. What we're gifted at – that's how he defined it.

That purpose, he explained, is what you were sent here to do ... your mission on Planet Earth.

But how does a person even get there? How do we figure out what our purpose is?

Easy. You try to identify what you can do better than anyone. Find that thing that's effortless. Discover what you're best at – and then do it like Hercules.

When people see you doing that, see you doing something better and more enthusiastically than anyone else, believe me ... it will be very obvious. You'll know you've found your purpose, your calling, and your mission in life.

The Quarantine Machine

Do you remember that quarantine time we had? Man, oh, man, I think everybody remembers those crazy days. Seems like almost everybody was nervous. Almost everybody was fearful. Almost everybody was so stressed out … about work, money, family … and, of course, that stupid virus!

But I say "almost everybody" for a reason.

My grandma and grandpa had a whole different reaction to all that mess during that crazy time. They call it the time they got down to business … and got to work!

They actually don't have jobs they go to anymore. They're retired. But they went to work at home … doing things they always wanted to do … but never got around to doing.

Grandpa started working on this woodworking project in the garage. He built a brand new bookcase. It looked amazing. Now he's building new cabinets for the kitchen.

And Grandma finally put all her recipes together and put them in the computer. Grandma's an incredible cook. And now she's going to publish her own cookbook!

I think my grandparents are super-smart. They took a negative situation and found something positive inside. And that's not easy to do … because most people I know just spent all that free time complaining!

There's Always a Way Out

Aunt Tammy told me this story about a truck driver with a big problem. He drove under this bridge one time and misjudged the height. His truck was too tall and that bridge was too short. His truck got stuck. It just kinda wedged in there and got all squished in underneath that bridge. He couldn't drive back out.

The drivers behind him started getting mad. And honking and screaming. And then the police came ... and the fire department. And they all stood around trying to figure out what to do. But nobody was doing anything. Not really.

Nobody wanted to cause more damage to that truck and that bridge. Aunt Tammy said they were just standing around talking about what a big mess it was ... how much everything was gonna cost ... and how much trouble that driver was in.

Then this lady was crossing the street with her five-year-old son. The little boy asked what happened. When the policeman explained the problem, the boy said, "Why don't they let the air out of the tires? Then the truck will be shorter ... and you can push it out. Then you put the air back in."

That policeman got a real surprised look on his face. And he said, "Wow. You got a good idea there, young fellow." And that's what they did. You see? Sometimes there's a very simple solution to what looks like a big, messy problem.

A lot of problems have simple solutions. Remember ... there's always a way out.

Ten Stupid Dollars

Today was a really good day. Best day of the year. I'm so happy. My father gave me the greatest gift I could ever have hoped for today.

Dad went to meet my Uncle Mickey. His baby brother, my Uncle Mickey. My favorite uncle. They met for lunch ... first time they've seen each other in years. Because my dad and my uncle had a big fight a long time ago ... when I was little.

I still remember that horrible day ... how they yelled and screamed at each other. I couldn't believe the terrible things they said. We all thought they were going to kill each other. It was that bad.

It was a stupid fight too. You know what it was about? Ten dollars. Ten stupid dollars one of them thought the other one was supposed to pay for something. They didn't speak for years because of those ten stupid dollars.

Yesterday, I asked my father if I gave him the ten dollars ... would he forgive my Uncle Mickey. Dad started crying ... first time I ever saw my father cry ... and then he picked up the phone and called his little brother. Today they met for lunch.

My mother says it best. We overcome evil with good. I heard her say that a million times. Yesterday, I tested it out on my father ... and I found out it's true. I think that's a lesson for all of us. Learn to forgive people. And never fight with people you love over stupid little things. Like ten stupid little dollars.

How Many Boxes?

My Uncle Eddie asked me to help him clean out his garage. Don't worry, he's paying me. Uncle Eddie never tries to take advantage. My favorite uncle.

We started last weekend and we're continuing this weekend. He needs help going through all his boxes. Uncle Eddie has a whole lot of boxes. You probably figured that part out already.

Uncle Eddie's moved around a lot and had a million different jobs. A million different hobbies too. Drawing, stamp collecting, calligraphy, doing magic tricks, reading comic books, all kinds of crazy exercise routines ... and lots of other things I never even heard of before. That's what's in all the boxes.

Some of that stuff has a lot of sentimental value for him ... and some of it is really just a bunch of old junk.

But Uncle Eddie has a hard time deciding which is which. That's where I come in. I help him organize, sort, clean, and toss.

It's hard for him to toss. He can never get rid of stuff. But how many boxes does a person need to be happy and live a good life? I told him, "It's not about the boxes, Uncle Eddie. Because even if you had zero boxes in your garage ... you'd still be my favorite uncle."

That Extra Three Cents

Did I ever tell you about my Uncle Artie? Uncle Artie is the greatest uncle ever. Totally awesome guy. Loved comic books when he was my age. He used to go to the candy store every Friday to buy the new comic books.

One day they raised the price of his comics from twelve cents to fifteen cents. Uncle Artie got real nervous. He started thinking, "How am I going to pay for this? Where am I going to get that extra three cents?"

He had a paper route at the time.

Woke up two hours early every day. Rode his bike all over the neighborhood delivering newspapers before school. He still only made a few dollars a week. Just a few dollars for all that work. And he still didn't know how to get that extra three cents.

But Uncle Artie worked hard and figured it out. He was always a hard worker, always looking for new opportunities.

Fast forward to today. Nowadays, Uncle Artie is one of the richest guys in town. Owns a bunch of different businesses. Every time he has a business problem … every time something goes wrong … he says he thinks back to that early problem … where was he going to get that extra three cents. Because solving that early problem taught him something … even though it was only three cents.

And today Uncle Artie still has to figure out how to pay for things. Except now … those things all have a lot more zeros in their price tag.

Similar and Very Different

My father owns a restaurant. Nice place ... with the best chicken sandwiches ever.

Anyway, there's these two guys working in the kitchen. They're dishwashers. Pretty hard job because it's very busy. There's always a million dishes to wash by hand.

These two guys are similar in one way – and different in another way. They don't speak English too well. They're from another country and haven't been here long. That's how they're similar.

In fact, they come from two small towns that are right next to each other. Very similar background. But one guy is kinda grumpy. He's the grumpiest grump of a grump. Doesn't talk nice to people. Doesn't help the other employees ... or the customers. A real sourpuss. Always complaining about how difficult it is to be in a new country ... and how hard it is to understand English.

The other dishwasher is the exact opposite. Friendly. Outgoing. Talks nice to everyone. Says he's so happy to be in a new country with more freedom and opportunity than where he was born. And he thinks English is difficult too, so he takes English classes early in the morning before work. Which must be pretty hard because he works pretty late.

But it just goes to show you. Two people. Same circumstances. Same background. But very, very different in the way they approach their external circumstances, environment ... and problems.

They're different on the outside because they're different on the inside. When you keep a good attitude on the inside, it affects everything on the outside. And that's a conscious choice we can all make. We can wake up every day and choose to be the grumpiest grump of a grump ... or we can wake up every day and choose to be very, very different.

It Started With a Joke

I can't stay long. I only have a minute. Gotta visit my best friends ... a brother and sister. They're both my best friends and they live next door.

I visit them a lot now. They're kinda going through a tough time. Their father left their mother. He moved out and got an apartment. He has another girlfriend, I guess. Kinda stinks, right?

Because my friends' parents had been together forever. Nobody could have predicted this. Nobody saw it coming. Their father met another lady at his job. They work together in the same store. People say that happens a lot to married couples. They meet someone new at their job. And before you know it, two new people are getting together ... and two other people are getting divorced.

But I can't agree with that explanation. I'm just a kid, but that's not how divorce works ... in my humble opinion. Nobody meets someone new and leaves the person they're married to right away.

It starts slowly. It starts with a joke. Then the joke becomes a little bit of flirting. Then it's a cup of coffee. Then it's lunch. Then it's dinner. Then it's divorce.

And a lot of people's lives get real messed up ... including little kids like my friends ... because someone acted like an idiot at their job. Remember, everything bad happens in steps. Nobody gets divorced right away. Next time you hear about some kid's parents splitting up ... you remember what I told you, okay?

It started with a joke.

Hot Coffee! Hot Coffee!

I can't believe what I just saw. This guy did the rudest thing. Rude times ten. And he should know better. Because he does know better. But he doesn't know that I know that he knows better.

It's ridiculous. He's a grown man with an important job and everything. A manager at my father's work. But he sure didn't act like a boss or any kind of manager today.

I went to work with my father, and I saw it. But you can listen and decide for yourself. All these people were waiting to get into the auditorium for a meeting, and this man came running through the crowd, yelling "Hot coffee! Hot coffee!"

Just like that. Real loud. So everybody moved out of the way and he squished himself through that line ... so he could be the first one in that auditorium.

And you guessed it ... there was no coffee. It was a trick, a fake-out, a lie just so he could get inside that auditorium first.

Sneaky, right? Obnoxious. Definitely unprofessional and not trustworthy. Because if he lies about a cup of coffee, what else will he lie about?

Maybe you think I'm making too much out of this. Maybe you think it's just a little thing. Maybe you think I'm complaining or gossiping. I disagree. I think it's important to point these things out when we notice them. Because there's an old saying. Little things don't mean a lot. They mean everything.

Keep it Down, Please!

We were working on an exercise in class. Just review questions for our test. Kinda like a practice test.

It's not being graded, but it was still kinda hard. I had to concentrate.

But it was so noisy outside our classroom! People were talking and joking and making all kinds of commotion right outside our door. Like they didn't even know a class was in session. Or they knew but didn't care!

Anyway, it was pretty hard to focus. Our teacher had to go outside and ask them to keep it down. She closed the door, but we could still hear them. Yapping and yapping away.

I couldn't believe people would keep talking like that when a class is in session right next to them! And I was wondering who these people were that didn't understand that kids have to study!

When the bell rang, we all walked out and I saw them. Still yapping away outside our door. And they weren't even kids. They were adults. And … believe it or not … they were teachers! Yeah, teachers who were there for a teachers' conference at our school. That got me really worried.

Because if teachers can act that way when they get together … would anybody really want teachers like that teaching their kids?

There's plenty of good teachers. I always had good teachers. Let's get the good teachers to teach those noisy teachers to keep it down, please.

Just One More ...

Just one more won't hurt. Right? Just one. I was watching a video. But then it ended ... and the next one popped up in the playlist. And it's hard to decide if I should click out or stay engaged.

But while I'm deciding ... or not deciding, actually ... the next episode starts playing right away. Before I know it, I find myself finishing that new episode and deciding whether to watch the next new one that pops up in the queue after that.

Then I'm still watching it two hours later. And meanwhile I had a ton of homework to do and a math test to study for.

All of a sudden, it's three hours later, my evening's gone, and it's time for bed. I say "all of a sudden," but it's not really "all of a sudden" because this happens every day.

I guess I'm kinda hooked ... on my technology and devices. I'm very aware of it. I'm not oblivious that something's happening. But I still wanna keep checking out all the new things that pop up.

Then this morning ... all of a sudden ... I decided to reboot my definition of "Just One More." From now on, it's just one more good habit, just one more dose of will power ... just one more way to make my own decisions ... instead of letting programmers make them for me. Starting today, I'm just one more straight-A student, just one more super-focused, super creative young person. Just one more kid who's paying attention. All of sudden.

Mike Kimmel

Working for the Census

My mom had a part-time job … with the Census. Do you know what that is? My dad calls it the Senseless … but that's a little disrespectful.

It's disrespectful to my mother … and to the Census. You know what it is, right? The Census is the big count. The big count the government does every ten years to total up all the people living in the country. I guess other countries must do the same thing too.

Except they don't call it the Census. And they definitely don't call it the Senseless. And it's important for the country – any country, really – to know how many people are there, what state and county they're in … how old they are … everything. That's how the government knows how many police and firemen they need, how many street lights, how much electricity … all kinds of stuff most people never even think about … because they assume the government is figuring it all out for them.

It's like … if we have a barbecue … we gotta know how many hamburgers to buy. But first we gotta know how many people are coming to our party.

So I think the Census is important … and I want to work for them like my mother did too. I guess next time they do it … I'll be a teenager … and I'll be old enough then. I'm pretty good with math, and I think I can do a good job helping our country count up all their people … just to make sure we don't lose anybody since the last Census.

Pavlov's Dogs

My school is doing something new. They started giving out "Skills Bills." They're like dollars ... except they're fake ones ... like play money.

Every time a teacher, teacher's aide, or counselor sees a kid doing something good, they hand them a Skills Bill.

The school calls it a Positive Reinforcement Learning Strategy. And the kids really like it too. It's makes kids feel like they got rewarded for doing something positive. And we can cash them in for prizes at the end of the month.

But my older brother says it's not a good idea. He's in college. He has a psychology class ... and learns about the way people think inside their minds.

My brother says it's like Pavlov's dogs. You know that story? Pavlov was a famous scientist who rang a bell every time he fed his dogs. Then he tried just ringing the bell ... without food ... and the dogs started salivating and getting happy and excited because they thought they were gonna eat. My brother says the Skills Bills are just like the bell Pavlov rang. A reward for good behavior that gets linked together in our mind. Just like Pavlov trained those dogs.

Well, you know what I say? I say, "So what?" Who cares what causes people to behave well ... as long as they behave well! That should really be the goal, shouldn't it? So give me a Skills Bill and ring the bell. Because I'm doing something good today!

The Recycling Center

I started recycling. Recycling all those little plastic bottles I used to throw away. And glass bottles too, because some of the healthy juices I like to drink come in glass instead of plastic.

I saw this movie about all the trash and plastic and junk that gets dumped everywhere and kills the animals and little fishies ... and it affected me. It made me wanna do something to help. To improve the situation ... and that's why I started recycling.

A couple of kids at school laughed. They made fun of me. They asked if I was poor. To tell you the truth, I didn't understand the question ... or why they were asking me that.

Then I realized it's because of the few dollars I get when I bring those bottles to the recycling center. Because that's what a lot of homeless people do to make a little bit of money to help keep themselves alive.

I know it's not a lot of money. It's not a lot of money to receive, but it's a small price to pay to save our planet. Or at least make our planet a little bit nicer place to live ... and breathe and walk and swim ... while we're trying to clean it all up. I don't know why anybody would wanna laugh at me for that.

The Junkyard

My Aunt Lisa taught me a lesson today. She picked me up and took me on a field trip ... to the junkyard.

I never thought I could learn anything at a place like that. But, boy, was I wrong.

Last place I thought I'd learn anything.

But Aunt Lisa says a good student can learn in all kinds of unusual situations. A bad student can't learn even if Albert Einstein was his teacher.

Well, the junkyard was definitely an unusual situation. There was old furniture, cars that used to be shiny and new, broken televisions, old computers. And a bunch of other stuff I didn't even recognize.

My Aunt Lisa said, "Stuff. It's all just stuff. And once upon a time it used to be all shiny and brand new."

I still wasn't quite understanding, but Aunt Lisa explained.

"Think of how people chased after this stuff to try and buy it when it was new. People saved money for it. Maybe some people stole money for it. Some people spent extra time at work instead of spending time with their families ... just to get this formerly-new stuff. And look at it all now. Junk."

Now I get it. So guess what I did today? Instead of bugging my parents for a new bike ... like I've been doing for the past month ... I spent the whole afternoon teaching my little sister to ride my old bike.

Mike Kimmel

Crows and Ravens

What's the difference between a crow and a raven? I'm serious. Where I live, there's crows and ravens. We have both. They look exactly the same. I can't tell them apart … even though I see a lot of them every day.

My little sister can tell them apart. She knows all about birds and animals. She knows which is which. One's an endangered species. I look at them and can't figure out which one's endangered and which one's un-endangered.

I have no idea. I still can't tell them apart. So it made me think, how many people can't tell us apart? I look like the other kids in my class. Same height, same size. Same … pretty much everything. Maybe one's a different skin color, maybe one has a little different hair, maybe one has different eyes. But we're pretty much the same. If a Martian came down from outer space, he'd look at us … and we'd look more similar than different.

Two eyes, two arms, two legs, one head, one nose. Some noses are bigger and honkier than others. But pretty much the same.

So, what's the difference between a crow and a raven? I can't tell, but probably nobody can tell the difference between you and one of your classmates, either.

So, do your best to be an individual. Try to stand out if you can. That makes people notice you. And if people notice you, make them notice you for a good reason, not a bad reason. That's what I learned from crows and ravens.

Every Life is Worthwhile

Do you ever look at homeless people on the street? I look at homeless people all the time.

A lot of people don't look. I look at them, and I stop and think, "You know, at one time, this person was my age. And before that, this person was even younger. Once upon a time, this person was a baby. Somebody's pride and joy." Maybe they were. If they came from a good home. I don't know. I never talked to them. But ... once upon a time ... that homeless person was somebody's dream baby. Somebody was so happy the day this person was born ... and look at them now.

How did they get like this? What happened? I'd like to find out. Because everybody is special and unique. Every life is worthwhile. But sometimes you look at somebody who's ... not in a good situation ... and you gotta try to remember them at their very, very best.

At one time, it was somebody's dream ... when this person came into the world. Now it's somebody's dream that they stay away from them ... don't sleep in front of their door ... make a great, big mess ... and scream crazy things out loud.

I wonder what happened to those sad, lost, lonely people. How they went from somebody's dream to where they are now ... sleeping on a piece of cardboard. Every day, I stop ... I look ... and I wonder about that. Because everyone has something to teach us ... and every life is worthwhile.

Don't Park Here

Nobody parks in front of Mr. Miller's house. He's that older gentleman who lives across the street. Well ... he's definitely older, but I'm not so sure you can call him a gentleman.

If someone makes the mistake of parking on the street in front of his house ... they never make that mistake again. Mr. Miller comes running outside, starts screaming, telling them to park somewhere else ... but not in front of his house. He even has this automatic spotlight in front of his house that shines in people's eyes if they try to park there.

Do you think this is a little weird? Well, I live across the street and I think it's a lot weird!

All the neighbors on our block know to keep their cars away from Mr. Miller's house. But every once in a while a stranger parks there. Boy, oh boy, do they get a rude surprise. Mr. Miller really gives them an earful.

I don't understand Mr. Miller. I thought grown-ups are supposed to know better, act better, do better, and be better. But instead, he starts fights with strangers over the stupidest, most insignificant little thing on the planet.

Maybe this is one of those lessons my mom and dad are wrong about. Older does not necessarily make you wiser.

Ambassador of Good

Did you ever wonder why you're here? I'm serious. Did you ever ask yourself what you're doing here?

I don't mean here in this room. I mean here on this planet. You. Me. All of us. Seriously. I'm not messing with you. Did someone send you here ... or is it all just random? Is there a higher power out there orchestrating every facet of our lives ... or is everything just a great big mish-mosh?

Some people believe in a Higher Power ... and some people believe in the Big Bang ... that everything exploded and came from nothing. Those are two completely different ideas. And there's really smart people on both sides. Teachers, college professors, and even scientists who tell you what they believe in ... and also tell you that the other side is wrong.

I understand that. What I don't understand is why some of them are so mean to each other ... the people who disagree with their point of view.

How about you? What do you believe? I'll tell you what I believe. I believe people should act nicer to each other ... no matter where we came from ... no matter how we arrived on this big, beautiful blue marble in space that all of us call home.

Let's just be nice to each other. Let's just start there.

A Texting Security Guard

I was with my mom at the bank. And ... I don't mean to complain about the security guard. But I'm gonna ... point out ... something about this security guard!

There's this lady security guard at the bank. And every time we go in there ... she's on her phone! She's texting ... or she's looking something up ... or scrolling through pictures! Or even making a call ... but mostly texting.

Now ... I'm not really scared and paranoid ... like some people ... that something's gonna happen. But if something's gonna happen ... if there's gonna be a bad guy ... there's a good chance it will be here ... in the bank! That's where they keep the money!

Which is why they have security guards in the bank. Like this lady. But I don't think she takes her job seriously. Not like she takes her texting seriously. I wish she would take the security of her customers more seriously ... at least as seriously as she takes her cell phone.

Well, I'll tell you this ... when I grow up and have my own bank account, I'm not gonna go to any bank with a security guard who plays on the phone. I want a big, tough mean looking security guard with a big, thick neck and a nasty attitude. So any bad guy who comes in will be scared away. Maybe a security guard with great big forearms like Popeye and a tattoo on his neck ... or her neck. It can be a female security guard. I'm not discriminating. As long as she's not texting.

Underestimated and Inspiring

I have to tell you about this lady who works in my school. She's amazing ... but completely underestimated by everyone ... and even disrespected sometimes. Can you believe this lady is an author? She wrote eleven books! Eleven books!

There's people out there who haven't *read* eleven books! I think that makes her some kind of a genius. Because she writes all these books while she's still working at the school for her regular job... which has nothing to do with her books, by the way.

Guess what her regular job is at school? No, she's not a teacher. Or the principal. Or even a guidance counselor. Those jobs would make sense for an author.

Give up?

She works as a custodian. She cuts the grass, takes out the garbage, cleans the classrooms, and fixes all the stuff that breaks. Custodians clean the bathrooms too.

You know what else? She wasn't even born in this country. English is not her first language. She didn't have a lot of education where she was born, but she makes the most of what she does have.

That's inspiring. She's underestimated by other people, but she's inspiring for me.

If she can write eleven books with a little bit of education, what can I do with a regular, normal education?

They Laughed at Him

Do you know who Alfred Adler is? Don't worry. Most people don't. Alfred Adler was famous in Psychology. That's the science of the mind. But when he was a kid, little Alfred failed a math test. No big deal, but his teacher told his parents he was bad at math.

That was wrong. There could be lots of reasons someone fails a test. But Alfred's teacher and his family never encouraged him in math after that. One day, his teacher put a difficult problem on the board and asked if anyone could solve it.

Only one kid raised his hand. Little Alfred Adler. The kid who's bad at math. The whole class laughed. Even the teacher laughed! But Alfred walked up to that board and solved that problem ... and everyone stopped laughing. See? They already decided he was bad at math. But that was in their minds, not in his reality.

Lots of famous people were laughed at. That's a good lesson. So don't worry if people laugh at you. If everyone's laughing, maybe it's because you're so smart ... and so advanced ... they can't understand how you think.

That means you're doing something right. You're on the right track. It's hard to be smart sometimes. Because some people won't understand you. And it's easier for them to laugh ... than to put on their thinking caps and try to figure out what you already understand.

I Was Just Pretending

There's this new kid at my school. Really sweet, but also really shy. Well, at least we all thought he was really sweet and really shy but we couldn't be sure because nobody could talk to him. We couldn't even make eye contact because he was always looking down. Right. At his phone. Always reading, texting, or swiping.

I know, I know, lots of kids do that, but this kid does it more than any other human being on the face of the Earth. Maybe on other planets too. In fact, he even bumped into people sometimes because he was texting while he was walking.

All my friends thought he was rude. But I wasn't convinced. I've met a lot of rude people in my lifetime, and he didn't seem to fit the pattern. I had a gut feeling he was just shy.

So I developed a plan. I started pretending to be on my phone all the time too. Somehow, this shy kid noticed me. Maybe our phones connected through the airwaves. He said hello. I guess he saw me on the phone all the time and thought to himself, "This kid is just like me ... this kid must be okay."

Maybe that wasn't honest. But when I think about all the things we pretend to be in life ... pretending to be on my phone to make a new friend is not such a bad thing to pretend.

Mike Kimmel

My Favorite Place

We had to write an essay for school. Not "My Summer Vacation," thank goodness. We do that one every year. This essay was about our favorite place ... our favorite place that we wanna go see in the future.

I picked Mount Rushmore. I always wanted to see Mount Rushmore, the giant statue with the four Presidents. It's in South Dakota. It's got George Washington, Abraham Lincoln, Thomas Jefferson, and Theodore Roosevelt.

It's so beautiful. I read a lot about it because I was interested. But you know what's most interesting about Mount Rushmore? If you look closely at George Washington ... you'll see they started to carve out his jacket, shirt, and tie.

But they didn't finish! They wanted to make the four Presidents ... from the waist up – not just the heads ... but didn't finish! And if you look closely at a picture of Mount Rushmore, you can see it today. There's a little outline of George Washington's jacket, shirt, and tie.

Mount Rushmore is incredible. But it's not perfect because it's not finished. That tells me something. When you do homework, play sports, take a test, or anything else ... you don't need to be perfect. Even if your work is not perfect, it can still be really good.

So the next time you're feeling a little down ... or unqualified, or think you're not doing well enough, just think about how beautiful Mount Rushmore is ... and think about our old friend George Washington, the Father of our Country, who never even got his jacket.

Conversation Cafe

In my school, they have an extra class. For students who were born in a different country. English is not actually their first language. It's their second language. That's why they call this class ESL ... for English as a Second Language.

The kids are from all different countries. Some speak Spanish. Some speak Russian, Armenian, French, Arabic, Hebrew, Farsi ... every different language you ever heard of. And some you never heard of.

They have one thing in common. They came here looking for a better life. Their families came for more freedom, more safety, more education, and more opportunity.

All different languages. All different reasons to be here. But they're all trying to learn English. They need to speak good English to do all the good things they came here to do.

That's why the school has this ESL class ... and they have extra practice during our lunch period. They call it the Conversation Cafe, where all the foreign students can practice speaking English. And kids born here can volunteer to help. That's what I started doing during lunch period, and I'm having a lot of fun. It helps these kids fit in and be comfortable here in our country ... and I'm learning a few foreign language words too.

That's good for me, good for the other students, good for the school, and good for the country.

Mike Kimmel

My Secret Identity

Can I tell you a secret? I have a secret identity. I can't tell the other kids at school. They wouldn't like it. And they wouldn't like me. So this has to stay a secret. Deal? Cool.

Here goes. I'm not like those other kids. I'm not interested in what they're interested in. When they talk about their video games ... sports ... or funniest TV shows, I tune out. Totally uninterested. Zero. But I pretend to be ... a little interested ... just to be polite and get along with others. It's important for people with secret identities to get along with people. So they don't suspect.

But after school, when I get home ... that's when I turn into my secret identity, The Artist. That's when I do all the things I *am* interested in doing. Art. Drawing. Painting. Coloring. Making comic books. Writing stories for my comic books. I love all that stuff.

I could write, draw, paint, and make comic books and cartoons all day. Those are my most favorite things when I become The Artist. And it doesn't matter what the other kids think ... because it's stuff I gotta do alone. If I don't draw my pictures, who's gonna draw them? Dr. Seuss? They're my pictures and my responsibility.

Sometimes having a secret identity is lonely. Because most artists work alone. And I don't expect the other kids to understand. But I don't want them to feel bad, either. So I'll keep pretending I'm a little interested in their stuff too. Just to get along with others ... and protect my secret identity.

Egg Salad Sandwiches

Did you ever have yourself a good old-fashioned egg salad sandwich? It's a simple thing to make ... not too hard to prepare at all. But there's just something about an egg salad sandwich that always makes me feel cool, calm, and collected.

Don't ask me to explain it, because I never understood it too well myself. But a simple white and yellow egg salad sandwich calms me down when I feel a little nervous or anxious.

I guess that's what they call a comfort food. Have you ever heard that expression? Comfort food. Know why they call it that? Because it provides comfort ... makes you feel comfortable. Almost like one of those emotional support dogs.

An egg salad sandwich has just the right mix of protein and carbs. Just the right mix of mushiness and firm consistency. It fills me all the way up to the top ... and makes me feel safe and warm and fuzzy. I know, I know, maybe I'm overthinking this whole concept of what an egg salad sandwich can be ... and can't be. Maybe the beneficial effect I receive is all in the mind. But isn't that where all comfort really comes from?

Our comfort always begins in the mind. My mom says the only thing that can bring you peace of mind ... is yourself. She's right, I guess.

But a good old-fashioned egg salad sandwich always seems to help.

An Old, Ugly Couch

I was driving with my dad and we saw another one of those big, ugly couches on the sidewalk. It was outside that old apartment building behind the library.

I never understood the concept of dumping an old couch on the sidewalk. Why would somebody even do that? First of all, it's so heavy! Who the heck wants to carry a big, old clunky couch outside if you don't even want it anymore? Who wants to do all that heavy lifting for something you want to get rid of anyway?

And besides – why just dump it? Somebody needs it. Somebody can use it. But nobody can use it if you leave it outside. The rain soaks it. The sun beats on it. Dogs go on it.

So what do you do? Glad you asked that question. You call up a charity group. A thrift store. A place that sells old furniture. They'll even come pick it up. So you don't have to carry it out.

My uncle had an old, ugly couch like that. He bought it at a thrift store. Had it for years. He loved it. But he wouldn't have it if somebody dumped it outside. Get it? Got it? Good.

So never dump an old, ugly couch outside. It's bad for your back. Bad for the environment. And it's bad manners too. I'm glad we had this little talk. Aren't you?

My Uncle's Weird Sense of Humor

What's the difference between ignorance and apathy? I don't know and I don't care. That's my Uncle Bill's joke. He thinks that's funny. In a weird, sarcastic kinda way.

He's definitely a little sarcastic, but not mean. Because he gets a little weird … and grumpy when he thinks people aren't acting smart. Aren't doing smart things with their lives.

Uncle Bill says people don't think. Some people just use their heads for a hat rack. Or to hammer nails into the wall. Ouch. But not for thinking. And that's what our heads were originally made for. For thinking up good stuff and thinking up solutions to all our problems in life.

And Uncle Bill can't stand it when people don't use their heads. That's why he uses his head to make up sarcastic jokes. Sometimes people say he's being a little mean … but you gotta understand his sense of humor.

In his own way, he's trying to give people a helping hand … through tough love. To help people do better. In his own … weird … sarcastic … tough love kinda way.

The Magic Show

My cousin did a magic show for my birthday. That was his present. I pretended I liked magic shows. I kinda do, actually. But I wouldn't care about seeing a magic show if my cousin wasn't the magician.

He's a real good guy. He's not really a magician, though. He's in high school. A little shy, but I think that's why he started doing these magic shows in the first place.

He does them everywhere. He did a show in the hospital for the patients. He went to a nursing home and did magic tricks for the senior citizens. Sometimes people pay him too.

But that's not why he does it. He says it helps him. It's good practice to get up in front of people ... and talk ... and present ... and get over his shyness. My cousin wants to be a teacher someday and he says it's good experience.

I think it's even better for the people who see his show. His magic tricks are not so great, actually. *What is great* is seeing this shy teenager going all over the place with his funny little bag of tricks ... trying to do something good with his life.

Teenagers have a bad reputation. People say they're lazy ... disrespectful ... always on their phones. But people would change their minds about teenagers if they met my cousin ... with his funny little bag of not-so-great magic tricks. He could change people's opinion about teenagers. And that's a pretty good magic trick. The very best magic trick he does.

Change for a Dollar

I was with my dad driving downtown. He was all stressed out. Again. Trying to find parking. That always stresses him out. He went around and around the block. Finally found a spot ... but didn't have change for the meter.

Dad didn't want to get a ticket. So he runs into this store. Hands the lady a dollar. And he asks – real polite, "Can you give me change for a dollar?" And you know what the lady says? She says, "Sorry, sir. I'm new here."

Dad says, "You're new here?! So what?! There's still four quarters in a dollar. That never changes! A dollar is always a dollar." Except Grandpa says a dollar's not worth what it used to be and won't even buy you fifty cents these days. Grandpa complains about the price of everything. But that's another story.

Back to my father. My dad loses it. Starts yelling and screaming at this poor lady. That big vein on his neck starts popping out. My mom always tells him to calm down. Dad never listens.

So Dad asks for the manager. Manager lady comes out. Talks real nice to him. Meanwhile, my father's still very upset. Manager explains, "It's Sunday, sir. The meters are free today. No tickets." Dad gets real quiet. Finally calms down. Just like magic.

And that's the kind of change I'd really like to see for a dollar. It would be worth a million dollars, actually. I'd like to see my dad calm down. I worry about my dad sometimes. But I know people can change. And I'd like to see my dad change into the kind of person who's calmer and more relaxed.

Free Donut Day

I'm really proud of my uncle. He loves donuts. He loves all kinds of sweets and desserts, but donuts are his most favorite. He's not super heavy, but he should probably lose a few pounds. And some of those pounds are definitely from his donuts.

Well, today was National Donut Day. Maybe International Donut Day. Some of the donut places were giving away free donuts. Well, my uncle was all over that!

He was watching me today, and he decided we should go get our free donut from his favorite donut shop. I like donuts too, but not like my uncle does. Just like any other normal, mortal human being likes donuts. My uncle said he was looking forward to this all week. Imagine looking forward to a free donut all week!

When we arrived, the line was around the block! Guess a few other folks had been looking forward to their free donuts all week too.

I thought … Oh, boy, we're gonna be in line all day. It looked like an hour wait for that free donut. What a dumb way to spend the afternoon!

But my uncle … kinda agreed. He didn't even park the car. He saw that line and turned around. He said let's forget it and go do something else. Like any other normal, mortal human being would.

I'm really proud of my uncle. He loves me more than he loves donuts.

Grandma Dyes Her Hair

Can I tell you a secret? My grandma dyes her hair. She's been dyeing it for years. Actually, I don't think it's a secret anymore. Everybody knows. Her hair is so dark. It looks exactly the same as it did in her wedding picture on the wall. Same exact style. Same exact color.

Grandma says she doesn't even know what her regular color is. Her natural color. Probably grey. Maybe white. But she likes to keep it the same as she did when she was younger. I don't know why. I think some grown-ups are sensitive about their looks, their hair, their wrinkles. Maybe I'll understand when I get older.

I can't speak for anybody else, but I think my grandma looks just fine. No matter what color her hair is, how many wrinkles she has … or how slowly she walks, either.

Can I tell you another secret? Me and her other grandchildren … we like our grandma just the way she is.

Even if she doesn't look the same as she did in her wedding picture.

"Act as if what you do makes a difference.
It does."

~ William James

Help Spread The Word

Thank you for purchasing this book. Thanks for reading all the way to the end too. I hope these monologues will prove helpful in all your auditions, rehearsals, and performances. Since writing **Scenes for Teens** back in 2014, it has been our goal to provide clean, practical, family-friendly monologues and scenes for young performers.

If you've enjoyed this book – and feel that it will benefit other young actors, their parents, and teachers – please consider posting a short book review on your favorite social media platform or book-related website. Book reviews are very important for authors. They help spread the word about an author's work to a broader audience, while increasing readership and visibility across multiple platforms.

Additionally, please consider recommending this book to your local public library or school. Schools and libraries can often purchase books at a significant discount. This will also assist in making this material available to young actors whose families may not be able to purchase copies for themselves.

About Ben McCain

Ben McCain is an actor and television news anchor who – among his many other roles – has played a wide variety of news anchors, reporters, and hosts in movies and television shows throughout his forty year career. He also plays politicians, law enforcement figures, and a broad range of good and bad guys. Ben has had recurring roles in two long-running television series, *Lois and Clark: The New Adventures of Superman* and Roger Corman's *Black Scorpion*.

As a host and anchor, Ben has interviewed Dr. Billy Graham, Ronald Reagan, Bill Clinton, Heather Locklear, Megan Mullally, Tim Allen, Tim Conway, Neil Patrick Harris, Tony Danza, Patrick Duffy, Antonio Sabato, Mariel Hemingway, Peter Onorati, Emma Samms, Johnny Cash, Waylon Jennings, Willie Nelson, Dolly Parton, Garth Brooks, Marty Stuart, Shania Twain, Chubby Checker, Dick Clark, and boxing greats Mike Tyson and George Foreman. Along with his brother, Butch, Ben hosted a popular morning television show in Oklahoma for twelve years. Brooks and James Marsden made their television debuts on the McCain Brothers' highly-rated program, *Good Morning Oklahoma*.

The McCain Brothers have also recorded 4 CDs and appeared on the television shows *Hee Haw, Good Morning America, All My Children, General Hospital* and *Loving*. They wrote and performed the theme song in the feature film *My Name Is Bruce* starring Bruce Campbell. Ben played the friendly, small town mayor in the Bruce Campbell project, and a news anchor in MGM's feature film *Bio-Dome*, starring Pauly Shore.

During the recent Coronavirus pandemic, Ben and his six-year-old son, Zac, produced more than 200 episodes of a YouTube show called ***Daddy and the Big Boy***. Ben continues to anchor live Covid-19 updates for Torrance CitiCable during the pandemic.

Ben and his bride Noelle tied the knot at the Little Brown Church in Studio City, California on December 4, 2010. Ben, Noelle, and Zac live in Los Angeles and also enjoy spending time on the family farm in Texas.

About Mike Kimmel

Mike Kimmel is a film, television, stage, and commercial ac-
tor and acting coach. He is a twenty-plus year member of
SAG-AFTRA with extensive experience in both the New York
and Los Angeles markets. He has worked with directors Francis
Ford Coppola, Robert Townsend, Craig Shapiro, and Christopher
Cain among many others. TV credits include *Game of Silence, Zoo,
Treme, In Plain Sight, Cold Case, Breakout Kings, Memphis Beat, Buffy
The Vampire Slayer,* and *The Oprah Winfrey Show.* He was a regular
sketch comedy player on *The Tonight Show,* performing live on
stage and in pre-taped segments with Jay Leno for eleven years.

Mike has appeared in dozens of theatrical plays on both
coasts, including Radio City Music Hall, Equity Library Theater,
Stella Adler Theater, Double Image Theater, The Village Gate,
and Theater at the Improv. He trained with Michael Shurtleff,
William Hickey, Ralph Marrero, Gloria Maddox, Harold
Sylvester, Wendy Davis, Amy Hunter, Bob Collier, and Stuart
Robinson. He holds a B.A. from Brandeis University and an
M.A. from California State University at Dominguez Hills.

He has taught at Upper Iowa University, University of New
Orleans, University of Phoenix, Glendale Community College,
Nunez Community College, Delgado Community College, and
in the Los Angeles, Beverly Hills, and Burbank, California public
school districts. He is a two-time past president of New Orleans
Toastmasters, the public speaking organization, and often serves
as an international speech contest judge.

Mike has written and collaborated on numerous scripts for stage and screen. *In Lincoln's Footsteps*, his full-length historical drama on Presidents Lincoln and Garfield, was a semi-finalist in the National Playwrights Conference at the Eugene O'Neill Theater Center. Mike also received the Excellence in Teaching Award from Upper Iowa University in 2014.

Mike is a full voting member of the National Academy of Television Arts and Sciences, the organization that produces the Emmy Awards. He is the author of **Scenes for Teens**, **Acting Scenes for Kids and Tweens**, **Monologues for Teens**, **Monologues for Kids and Tweens**, **One-Minute Monologues for Teens**, **Monologues for Teens II**, and **Six Critical Essays on Film: A College Guide for Film Appreciation**.

In 2019, the Independent Author Network selected Mike's third published book, **Monologues for Teens**, as their Performing Arts Book of the Year. He is also featured and pictured in Francis Ford Coppola's groundbreaking 2017 book, **Live Cinema**.

"Let us not tire of a good work, hard though it be and wearisome; think of the many little hearts that in their sorrow look to us for help."

~ Louisa May Alcott

CPSIA information can be obtained
at www.ICGtesting.com
Printed in the USA
LVHW011304230821
695886LV00003B/317